THE SIMPLE SMALL BATCH BAKING COOKBOOK

ALICE E WEBSTER

Copyright © 2023 Alice E Webster

All rights reserved.

INTRODUCTION

Welcome to "The Simple Small Batch Baking Cookbook," your one-stop guide to creating delicious, perfectly-portioned baked goods in the comfort of your own home. Whether you're a seasoned baker looking to explore new recipes or a beginner eager to learn the basics, this cookbook offers an array of mouthwatering recipes that cater to every skill level and taste.

Small batch baking is a fantastic way to satisfy your cravings without making an excessive amount of food. It's perfect for those who live alone, couples, or small families, as well as for anyone who wants to try out different recipes without the worry of leftovers going to waste. This cookbook is designed to help you master the art of small batch baking while exploring a variety of flavors and techniques.

In Chapter 1, we'll introduce you to small batch baking and provide helpful tips and tricks to make your baking experience enjoyable and stress-free. We'll cover essential tools, ingredient substitutions, and storage solutions, setting you up for success from the start.

Chapter 2 dives into the world of breads and biscuits, with recipes ranging from Honey Whole-Wheat Loaf and Hawaiian Potato Dinner Rolls to Chorizo Cheddar Cornmeal Biscuits and

Parmesan, Rosemary, and Olive Focaccia. These comforting and flavorful recipes will soon become staples in your home.

As you progress to Chapter 3, you'll discover delightful muffins and cupcakes that are perfect for breakfast, dessert, or a midday treat. Indulge in Lemon Poppy Seed Sour Cream Muffins, Pumpkin Walnut Muffins, or Earl Grey Cupcakes with Rosemary-Honey Frosting, among many other delectable options.

Chapter 4 is all about cookies, brownies, and bars. Whether you crave the classic taste of Buttery Shortbread or the irresistible combination of sweet and salty in Brown Butter Chocolate Chip Cookies with Sea Salt, these recipes are sure to satisfy your sweet tooth.

In Chapter 5, we present an assortment of cakes and shortcakes that are perfect for celebrations or just because. From elegant Almond Olive Oil Cake with Honey-Thyme Glaze to whimsical S'mores Layer Cake, there's something for every occasion and palate.

Chapter 6 takes you on a journey through pies, tarts, and quiche. Master the art of homemade pie crusts, and then fill them with scrumptious ingredients like Cherry Pistachio Streusel, Hazelnut Chocolate Caramel, or savory Mushroom, Spinach, and Feta. These recipes will elevate your baking repertoire to new heights.

For fans of puddings and cheesecakes, Chapter 7 is a dream come true. Whip up silky Chocolate Pots de Crème, indulge in No-Bake Mini Vanilla Cheesecakes with Strawberry Compote, or savor the richness of Spiced Pumpkin Cheesecake with Gingersnap Crust. These desserts are sure to impress.

Finally, in Chapter 8, we explore turnovers and pastries that make for delightful breakfasts, snacks, or desserts. Savor the sweetness of Cinnamon Apple Turnovers, the savory goodness of Cremini Mushroom, Thyme, and Gruyère Turnovers, or the flaky perfection of Easy Kouign-Amann.

With "The Simple Small Batch Baking Cookbook" as your guide, you'll embark on a journey filled with delicious baked goods that can be enjoyed without the worry of excess leftovers. We've taken the guesswork out of scaling down recipes so you can focus on what truly matters: enjoying the process of baking and savoring your creations. Happy baking!

As you explore the recipes in "The Simple Small Batch Baking Cookbook," you'll not only expand your culinary horizons but also develop your skills and confidence in the kitchen. Small batch baking is a fantastic way to experiment with new flavors and techniques, and this cookbook will be your trusted companion throughout your journey.

One of the unique aspects of small batch baking is its focus on mindfulness and intentionality. Baking smaller quantities encourages us to slow down, savor each step, and appreciate the process as much as the end result. This mindful approach can enhance your overall baking experience and even transform it into a meditative, stress-relieving activity.

In addition to the wide variety of recipes, this cookbook also offers practical advice on how to modify or scale recipes based on your needs. You'll learn how to adjust ingredient quantities, baking times, and temperatures, ensuring that your small batch creations turn out perfectly every time.

Moreover, small batch baking is an eco-friendly and budget-conscious choice. By making smaller quantities, you'll reduce food waste and save money on ingredients. Plus, since many of the recipes in this cookbook use readily available, everyday ingredients, you'll be able to create delicious treats without breaking the bank.

As you progress through the chapters, don't be afraid to experiment and make these recipes your own. Feel free to substitute ingredients based on your preferences or what's available in your pantry. The beauty of small batch baking is its flexibility and adaptability, allowing you to create unique and personalized treats that cater to your taste buds.

In addition to the recipes themselves, this cookbook also includes a handy Measurement Conversions section to help you easily switch between metric and imperial measurements, ensuring accuracy and ease in your baking endeavors.

It's our hope that "The Simple Small Batch Baking Cookbook" becomes a cherished resource in your kitchen, inspiring you to create and share delicious, perfectly-portioned baked goods with your loved ones. Whether you're a seasoned baker or a novice, these recipes are designed to bring joy, satisfaction, and a sense of accomplishment as you master the art of small batch baking.

So, preheat your oven, gather your ingredients, and let's get started on this exciting journey. With "The Simple Small Batch Baking Cookbook" by your side, you'll soon discover the endless possibilities and unparalleled joy that small batch baking has to offer. Happy baking, and bon appétit!

As you delve deeper into "The Simple Small Batch Baking Cookbook," you'll notice that the recipes have been carefully curated to cater to a variety of palates and dietary preferences. From wholesome breads and biscuits to decadent cakes and pastries, there's something for everyone in this collection of small batch recipes.

One of the primary advantages of small batch baking is the ability to cater to individual preferences and dietary needs. If you or someone in your household has dietary restrictions, such as a gluten sensitivity or dairy intolerance, you can easily adapt these recipes to meet those specific needs without the risk of wasting large quantities of ingredients. This cookbook offers suggestions for substitutions and adjustments, making it a versatile and inclusive guide for all bakers.

Small batch baking is also an excellent choice for those living alone or in small households. You no longer have to worry about leftovers going stale or having to eat the same dessert for days on end. By baking in smaller quantities, you can enjoy a variety of fresh, homemade treats throughout the week without feeling overwhelmed by an abundance of baked goods.

Moreover, small batch baking offers a unique opportunity to experiment with new flavor combinations and techniques without committing to a large batch. If you've ever been hesitant to try a new recipe because of the fear of failure or waste, small batch baking is the perfect solution. It allows you to test new ideas and learn from your experiences with minimal risk.

Not only is small batch baking a practical and versatile approach to creating delicious treats, but it also fosters a sense of connection and togetherness. By sharing these thoughtfully crafted, homemade goodies with friends and family, you're not only offering a delicious treat but also expressing your love and care through the time and effort you've invested in creating something special.

As you embark on your small batch baking journey, remember to have fun and enjoy the process. Embrace your creativity and don't be afraid to experiment with different ingredients, techniques, and flavors. The beauty of small batch baking lies in its adaptability and the endless possibilities it offers.

We hope "The Simple Small Batch Baking Cookbook" becomes a treasured guide and source of inspiration as you explore the world of small batch baking. Here's to many delightful baking adventures and the unforgettable memories you'll create along the way. Happy baking!

CONTENTS

CHAPTER 1: Welcome to Small Batch Baking 1

CHAPTER 2: Breads and Biscuits 22

Honey Whole-Wheat Loaf

Hawaiian Potato Dinner Rolls

Brioche Hamburger Buns

Rosemary Goat-Cheese Biscuits

Chorizo Cheddar Cornmeal Biscuits

Parmesan, Rosemary, and Olive Focaccia

Mock Sourdough English Muffins

Sesame Seed and Onion Bagels

CHAPTER 3: Muffins and Cupcakes 42

Lemon Poppy Seed Sour Cream Muffins

Pumpkin Walnut Muffins

Banana Blueberry Muffins

Peach Streusel Muffins

Lemon Meringue Cupcakes

Classic Yellow Cupcakes with Chocolate Fudge Frosting

Chocolate Cupcakes with Peanut-Butter Pretzel Frosting

Strawberry Cupcakes with White Chocolate Cream Cheese Frosting

Earl Grey Cupcakes with Rosemary-Honey Frosting

CHAPTER 4: Cookies, Brownies, and Bars 66

Almond-Butter Cookies

Buttery Shortbread

Brown Butter Chocolate Chip Cookies with Sea Salt

Chai-Spiced Snickerdoodles

Double Chocolate Chunk Brownies

Peanut Butter Blondies

Carrot Cake Bars with Cream Cheese Swirl

Raspberry Oatmeal Almond Crumb Bars

Millionaire Shortbread Bars with Caramel and Chocolate Ganache

CHAPTER 5: Cakes and Shortcakes 88

Almond Olive Oil Cake with Honey-Thyme Glaze

Chocolate Cake with Raspberry Jam Filling

Buttermilk Roulade Cake with Mascarpone Berry Filling

Sticky Toffee Pudding Cake with Bourbon Toffee Sauce

S'mores Layer Cake

Chocolate Lava Cakes

Strawberry Shortcakes with Lemon Whipped Cream

Whole-Wheat Oat Shortcakes with Apples and Whipped Cream

CHAPTER 6: Pies, Tarts, and Quiche 115

Brown Sugar Butter Pie Crust

Everything but the Bagel Pie Crust

Cherry Pistachio Streusel Pie

Mini Pumpkin Pies

Greek Yogurt Berry Tart

Hazelnut, Chocolate, and Caramel Tart

Strawberry Rhubarb Mini Galette

Mini Pizza Quiche with Pepperoni, Mozzarella, and Olives

Mini Bacon and Cheese Quiche

Mushroom, Spinach, and Feta Quiche

CHAPTER 7: Puddings and Cheesecakes 140

Chocolate Pots de Crème

Classic Vanilla Bean Crème Brûlée

Banana Cream Pudding Parfaits

Tiramisu

No-Bake Mini Vanilla Cheesecakes with Strawberry Compote

Spiced Pumpkin Cheesecake with Gingersnap Crust

Brownie-Bottom Turtle Cheesecake Bars

Butterscotch Pudding

CHAPTER 8: Turnovers and Pastries 162

Cinnamon Apple Turnovers

Blueberry Thyme Turnovers

Egg and Cheese Breakfast Turnovers

Cremini Mushroom, Thyme, and Gruyère Turnovers

Cinnamon Rolls

Apricot and Raspberry Jam Kolaches

Easy Kouign-Amann

Brie, Fig, and Pine Nut Danish

Measurement Conversions.. 183

CHAPTER 1
welcome to small batch baking

If you are looking for a pie recipe, it's very easy to find one. However, if you live in a household with just one, two, or three people, you'll end up with leftovers for days.

This is not your regular baking cookbook. Gone are the days where you're stuck making a dozen or more cupcakes when that chocolate craving hits, when you only actually want four. No longer will you have to work out confusing measurement conversions. This book is here to solve those problems with simple, delicious recipes that are scaled down for you.

A Primer on Small Batch Baking

Small batch baking simply means making a small batch of something. For most recipes here, the yield is six servings. But you won't need to purchase any specialty mini bakeware; these recipes will use the standard baking pans you likely already have in your kitchen.

In this chapter I'll go through the equipment you need for these recipes, the staples you'll want to keep in your kitchen, and everything else you'll need to know about what goes into small batch baking. I'll also cover some easy hacks to get you the perfect yield for whatever you are creating.

SMALL BATCH BASICS

Small batch baking isn't just dividing a normal recipe in half—a lot more goes into it. The recipes in this book are specifically written to produce a smaller amount of dessert. Sure, cookies and cupcakes won't have much more to them than a smaller number. However, when it comes to constructing a layered cake, I'll show you how to do it using only standard kitchen equipment so you end up with six elegant slices.

BENEFITS OF SCALING DOWN

Here are a few benefits of small batch baking:

- » Satisfy your cravings without having too much left over or wasting food.
- » Enjoy your bakes while they're still nice and fresh.
- » Cook efficiently for smaller dinners, celebratory events, and get-togethers.
- » Try out a new recipe without making a lot of something you may not like.

A NOTE ON RECIPE YIELDS

The recipes in this book are scaled down to reach specific yields—usually six servings and sometimes four. I set these yields for ease and convenience. In each chapter, you'll find similar desserts that will have the same yield. Every recipe can be either halved or doubled, if needed.

In the breads and biscuits chapter, you'll get a yield of six servings. These savory pieces of dough are the perfect amount to accompany a family dinner, with minimal or no leftovers. Cupcakes and muffins will have a yield of six. These delectable treats are the perfect number for a Sunday breakfast or an afternoon treat. Cookies will give you the highest yield—12 cookies. I've done this specifically because I, for one, will never eat just one cookie. Brownies and bars will give you a yield of six.

Cakes and shortcakes are designed for smaller gatherings, giving you a yield of six slices for each. Pies, tarts, and savory quiche will give you a yield of six—that's right, no more making an entire cherry pie when all you want is dessert for your small family.

Cheesecakes will give a yield of six, while puddings will yield four. Why the smaller number? Well, most of us have a set of four ramekins, so it seemed more appropriate. Yes, I've thought about this a lot.

Finally, pastries and turnovers will give you a yield of six. Frankly, I'll likely eat all six myself, but you can share if you like.

Your Small Batch Kitchen

If you already bake a little, you probably have the necessary bowls and pans to make all the recipes in this book. I am a professional pastry chef, and I can tell you I only have standard baking equipment in my home. There's really no need for any kind of specialty equipment—especially not for small batch baking.

ESSENTIAL BAKEWARE

It can be frustrating to have to go out and buy a new pan just for one recipe. Often, this specialty bakeware then gets stored away collecting dust until *maybe* a year later when you feel the urge to try that recipe again. And that's just a maybe. But you won't need any special mini bakeware for this book. Let's go through the list of what you will need.

- **Muffin tin:** You'll need a standard muffin tin for muffins, cupcakes, mini pies and quiche, buns, and some pastries. A six-cup is all you need, but if you already have a 12-cup, that's fine; you'll just fill half the cups.

- **Loaf pan:** This multiuse pan is not only great for making loaves of bread, it also is a perfect size to make small batch brownies, bars, and cakes. I use this pan a lot, so I have several in my kitchen. They come in a few sizes. The standard size, and the one used in this book, is 9 by 5 inches.

- **8-inch-square baking pan:** This 8-by-8-inch pan is handy for small batch pies, cakes, and even cinnamon rolls. I bet some of you have this pan in your kitchen and have no idea where it came from. It's that common!

- **Baking pan:** This rectangular 9-by-13-inch pan is not just for casseroles and lasagna. The size is perfect for constructing a small batch layer cake. We'll even use it to create a water bath for custards in chapter 7.

- **Sheet pan:** This common piece of bakeware comes in many sizes. The size of your sheet pan is not really important, just as long as you have one. I use a standard jelly roll size that is 11 by 15 inches. This pan is used for things like cookies, biscuits, breads, pastries, and turnovers.

- **Mixing bowls:** You'll need some good mixing bowls. They come in metal, plastic, or glass. Any material will work just fine. Small, medium, and large would be preferable, but at least make sure some bowls are large so you have plenty of room to mix.

- **Ramekins:** These little dessert dishes usually come in a set of four, in various sizes. The common sizes are usually 4-ounce or 6-ounce, and the recipes in this book are designed to fit in that range. These ramekins will need to be either glass or ceramic and oven-safe, so plastic ones will not work.

» **Measuring cups and spoons:** These are necessary for any recipe. Plastic or metal is fine; that's more of a personal preference. A good liquid measuring cup is also great to have, and a small one yielding 1 cup is all you'll need.

» **Wire cooling rack:** You'll need this for cooling your baked goods evenly when they come out of the oven. The perfect bake always needs to cool down properly for the best results. Since we'll be making small batches, you'll only need one rack.

» **Stand mixer or electric hand mixer:** Not all the recipes in this book will require the use of a hand mixer or a stand mixer, but some will. Recipes like bread and buttercream frosting *can* be made by hand, but they come together much more easily when you use a mixer. Stand mixers sit on top of a table or counter and come with a bowl and various attachments. They are more of an investment, so if you already have one, great. Otherwise, electric hand mixers are a perfect, inexpensive substitute. For the recipes in this book, you can use them interchangeably.

» **Spatula and whisk:** For the recipes that can be made by hand in one bowl, you'll need a spatula and a whisk. I personally like silicone spatulas that are heat-proof, and I use various sizes. As for the whisk, a small one will do just fine. You'll want sturdy prongs and a nice handle for gripping.

» **Kitchen scale:** This tool is totally optional. All of the recipes in this book have both volume and weight measurements, so it's up to you if you want to pull out the scale for weight precision. A kitchen scale is inexpensive, and you can easily find a great one on baking websites or Amazon.

BAKEWARE HACKS

Here are some easy hacks to get the most out of your standard bakeware.

- **Use a 9-by-13-inch baking pan to create a small layer of cake.** Once baked and cooled, cut that cake into four equal squares and layer it with your favorite frosting.
- **Make mini pies in a muffin tin instead of your pie pan.** The process is the same as making a standard pie, but you'll end up with cute little personal pies.
- **Use a loaf pan to make a small batch of brownies, blondies, or cookie bars—or a layer cake.** Simply bake the cake in a loaf pan, cool it on a wire rack, and then cut it in half across. Layer the cake with your favorite filling.
- **Use a 9-by-13-inch baking pan instead of a jelly roll pan for roulade cakes.** The process is basically the same; just bake and cool the cake and then roll it up with your favorite filling inside.
- **An 8-inch-square pan is a great option to scale down your favorite pie, tart, or quiche.** It's just as easy to use as a standard pie pan.

PANTRY STAPLES

Before you start baking, you'll need to stock your kitchen with some common baking ingredients. These are easy to find at any grocery store, and each has a very long shelf life. These dry ingredients are not perishable and can be stored away in your pantry. I use airtight, sealed containers for my pantry staples. They look nice and tidy with each one filled with its own ingredient, and the lid keeps everything fresh.

FLOUR

Flour is used in almost all of these recipes. Most of the recipes call for regular all-purpose flour, which is great for everything from cakes to cookies and even bread. In some recipes, you'll find whole-wheat flour. This imparts a slightly sweet and nutty taste but can easily be swapped for all-purpose if you prefer. Flour should be stored in a cool, dry area, preferably in an airtight container.

GRANULATED SUGAR

White granulated sugar is the main sweetener in just about every recipe. It comes in boxes and bags ranging from 2 to 25 pounds, and it's up to you which to get. Granulated sugar should be stored in a dry area in an airtight container, if possible, to avoid humidity and clumping.

POWDERED SUGAR

Powdered sugar is also known as confectioners' sugar. This ingredient is most common in frostings and glazes. Powdered sugar is finely ground sugar, and just the slightest bit of humidity can make it clump up. For this reason, I recommend that you store it in an airtight container and sift it before use.

BROWN SUGAR

Brown sugar is made by combining molasses and white sugar, so it is wetter than the other dry ingredients. It's another ingredient that does not do well with humidity and can easily dry out as well, so storing it in an airtight container will prevent both drying out and clumping. If your brown sugar does dry out, you can bring it back to life by putting a slice of bread into the airtight container with the brown sugar overnight. The moisture from the bread will soften up your dried-out brown sugar. Either light brown sugar or dark brown sugar will work well for these recipes.

UNSWEETENED COCOA POWDER

Cocoa powder comes in a few different forms: natural cocoa, Dutch-process cocoa, and black cocoa. Each of them is a different shade of brown, and each imparts a slightly different flavor. While all of them would work great in any of these recipes, the most commonly found, and the one I use most, is natural cocoa powder. Keep it in a dry area in an airtight container.

VANILLA EXTRACT

Pure vanilla extract just cannot be beat. A little bit will bring great flavor to your baked goods. I buy vanilla paste, which is vanilla extract with vanilla beans in it. It's a little more expensive than extract, but imparts a much bigger vanilla punch. Vanilla should be kept in a cool, dry area in your pantry.

LEAVENING

Leavening includes both baking soda and baking powder. Both of these are used to get the best rise out of your baked goods. Both can be stored in a dry and cool area of your pantry in the containers they are purchased in. Be mindful that these types of leavening are best used fresh, so if you've had the same baking soda in your cabinet for more than 10 years, it may be time to buy a new box.

SALT

A lot of people don't think about salt when it comes to baking, but salt actually is crucial for a perfectly balanced treat. A little salt goes a long way when it comes to sweets. I use kosher salt in all my bakes because the salinity is not as strong as iodized and sea salt. Along with all the rest of the dry ingredients, salt should be stored in an airtight container in a dry and cool area.

CANOLA OIL

Some recipes call for canola oil instead of butter. It makes for a lighter crumb for cakes and cupcakes. You can actually use any vegetable oil. Store it in the original container in a dry and cool area in your pantry.

REFRIGERATOR AND FREEZER STAPLES

To bake any recipe, you'll need a combination of wet and dry ingredients. We've just gone over the dry, so let's talk about what wet ingredients you'll want to stock in your refrigerator before you start your small batch bakes. Wet ingredients are perishable, which is why they are kept in the refrigerator. For each item, you'll want to buy the minimal amount needed so it does not go to waste before you can complete your baking. In this section I'll also provide some ingredient substitutions and discuss ways to stretch your products' shelf life.

BUTTER

Unsalted butter is always the way to go. I prefer to control the level of salinity in my baked goods, which is why I always buy unsalted butter. If all you have is salted butter, though, just reduce the amount of salt in the recipe. Butter should be kept in the refrigerator unless the recipe calls for room-temperature butter. In that case, let the butter come to room temperature overnight before baking. To stretch the shelf life of butter, you can store it in the freezer until needed.

EGGS

Eggs usually come in cartons of 6, 12, or 18. You always want to open the package and make sure none are broken before selecting your carton at the store. Eggs should always be stored in the refrigerator. If the recipe calls for an egg white or yolk, you can save the other part of the egg for another recipe in a sealed container in the refrigerator for up to one week.

MILK

For the most flavorful baked goods, full-fat dairy milk is the best choice. The milk fat provides richness to your final baked goods. If you're buying milk for the family and usually go with a different variation or less fat, you can always use that for your baked goods as well. It will not hinder the recipe results in any way. Milk should always be stored in the refrigerator.

BUTTERMILK

Buttermilk is one of those things that is fantastic in baked goods but is rarely used for anything else. If you do not want to buy a carton of buttermilk, you can easily make it at home by using whole or 2 percent milk and squeezing in some fresh lemon juice. The acid from the lemon juice will curdle the milk, giving your baked goods that tangy flavor. Store buttermilk in the refrigerator.

SOUR CREAM

If you ever wonder why a cake or muffin is so moist, it probably has sour cream in the batter. It's used in a variety of baked goods, and keeping a pint in your refrigerator is a good way to be ready for small batch baking. If you don't have it, you can use either mayonnaise or plain Greek yogurt; both are great substitutes.

CREAM CHEESE

This versatile ingredient is used for frostings, cheesecakes, and glazes. It has a long shelf life when stored in the refrigerator. When you are getting ready to bake, cream cheese needs to come to room temperature before being used. I like to buy the blocks of plain cream cheese rather than the flavored types.

ACTIVE DRY YEAST

Yeast comes in many forms: instant yeast, fresh yeast, and active dry yeast. The kind most commonly found at grocery stores, and the one used in the recipes in this book, is active dry yeast. An unopened package of yeast can be kept at room temperature, but for a longer shelf life, I always keep yeast in the refrigerator. If the package is opened, transfer the contents to a sealed container for optimal freshness. Different yeasts have different strengths. If you can only find instant yeast or fresh yeast in your area, a quick Google search will help you convert the quantity you need for these recipes.

LEMONS

Although lemons are used only in some baked goods, I like to keep them on hand as a general staple. Whether it be for zest or just a drop of lemon juice, lemons are a great ingredient that comes in handy more often than you might think. I keep them in the crisper drawer of my refrigerator for the longest shelf life.

SHOPPING FOR SMALL BATCH BAKING

Sometimes you'll already have the ingredients needed to complete your small batch bakes. Sometimes, however, you may not. In this section, I'll cover the best plan of action before you go shopping.

PLAN AHEAD.

Have a shopping list before heading to the store so you don't end up buying things you don't actually need. Look at each recipe you're planning to make, and jot down the common ingredients among them. Think about how much of each ingredient you'll need and plan accordingly. I recommend making a list.

BUY IN BULK.

If you plan on doing a lot of baking, all dry ingredients can be purchased in bulk. Items like butter can be also purchased in bulk and kept in the freezer. Canned ingredients such as sweetened condensed milk and pumpkin puree can be bought in bulk and, if unopened, will last just about forever. Ingredients like sugar and flour are going to be used the most. Grocery stores offer a lot of different sizes to buy, so make sure what you are buying can fit into the container you have to store it in.

BUY FRESH.

Unlike sugar and flour, ingredients like fruit don't have a long shelf life. When you are ready to make a recipe that contains an ingredient like blueberries or peaches, try to pick out the fruit that feels firmest. This way, you will likely have a day or two to spare before the fruit gets too ripe and mushy. Also, firmer fruits generally hold up better in baked goods.

CHECK DATES.

It's important to check the sell-by dates on all things dairy. The last thing anyone wants is to start their baking project only to realize their milk has spoiled. Believe it or not, grocery stores sometimes miss when there is old milk left out on the shelves. It's always a good idea to double-check the sell-by date.

COMPARE PRICES.

Grocery costs can add up quickly, so it's a great idea to compare prices. Instead of grabbing just any bag of flour, compare prices to see how much other brands cost. Don't get me wrong—quality ingredients are important—but I recommend that you spend your money on ingredients where quality is most important, like chocolate and butter.

LEFTOVER INGREDIENTS AND WHAT TO DO WITH THEM

Unfortunately, baking will undoubtedly lead to leftover ingredients—things in cans, spices, and even some perishable items. In this section, I'll go over what those items may be and give you suggestions for how you can use them up.

BUTTERMILK

Buttermilk is one of those ingredients that is commonly bought for the sole purpose of being baked into something. If you find yourself with leftover buttermilk, there are many other ways to use it up. Try making a buttermilk-ranch dressing or buttermilk pancakes. Buttermilk can also be used as a marinade for some fried chicken, as it helps tenderize the meat. Buttermilk can be mixed with mayonnaise and vinegar and tossed with some cabbage the next time you're making coleslaw or potato salad. Alternatively, you can use buttermilk to make Chocolate Cupcakes with Peanut-Butter Pretzel Frosting or Chorizo Cheddar Cornmeal Biscuits. Buttermilk has an expiration date and should be kept in the refrigerator until that date.

EGGS

You'll find a lot of recipes in this book that call for one egg white or one egg yolk, which means you'll likely end up with some leftovers. Don't waste these! I love to save egg whites to make myself an egg-white omelet filled with vegetables and cheese. Egg whites are also great to make a quick meringue topping for a bowl of fruit. If you're feeling fancy, you can use your leftover egg white as a whipped foam garnish on a cocktail. If you have leftover egg yolks, those have many uses as well. Save the yolk and add it to your next egg scramble for a little more richness. Egg yolks can be whipped into a hollandaise sauce, or you can use one to make homemade mayonnaise. Some great recipes for leftover egg parts are Brown Butter Chocolate Chip Cookies with Sea Salt and Lemon Meringue Cupcakes.

SOUR CREAM

Sour cream is a versatile ingredient that you can use in various ways if you find yourself with leftovers. I always have sour cream in my refrigerator because I am partial to putting it on my baked potatoes. Sour cream can also be mixed with lime juice to make a zesty, creamy taco topping or mixed with eggs to make the fluffiest scrambled eggs ever. It can be used to make a creamy sauce for beef stroganoff or even mixed into some marinara to make it extra rich. You can use it to replace mayonnaise in just about anything and even replace the milk in some baked recipes. Other ways to repurpose leftover sour cream can be to make [Lemon Poppy Seed Sour Cream Muffins](#) or [Classic Yellow Cupcakes with Chocolate Fudge Frosting](#).

SWEETENED CONDENSED MILK

Leftover sweetened condensed milk can be used for a variety of things, including as a sweetener in coffee, tea, or hot chocolate. Thai iced tea is a strong tea that is best when mixed with sweetened condensed milk. My personal favorite way to repurpose sweetened condensed milk is by making whipped cream with it. Try this out for the [Millionaire Shortbread Bars with Caramel and Chocolate Ganache](#). Leftover sweetened condensed milk should be kept in a sealed container and stored in the refrigerator.

PUMPKIN PUREE

The smallest can of pumpkin puree you can buy is 15 ounces. That means you'll likely have leftovers after your small batch pumpkin bakes. My favorite way to repurpose leftover pumpkin puree is to make a pumpkin banana smoothie. Simply blend the puree with 1 banana, ½ cup of yogurt, ½ teaspoon of cinnamon, ½ teaspoon of ground ginger, and ½ cup of milk and enjoy! Other great ways to repurpose your pumpkin is to mix it into pancake batter or combine it with some whipped cream to top a bowl of berries. Pumpkin is great mixed into a hearty bowl of chili or cooked down with some herbs and chicken stock to make a pumpkin soup. I personally like to make my own pumpkin latte by adding a spoonful of puree along with cinnamon and ginger to taste in my regular coffee. You can also use pumpkin puree to make Pumpkin Walnut Muffins or Spiced Pumpkin Cheesecake with Gingersnap Crust. If you have leftover puree, transfer it to an airtight container and store it in the refrigerator for up to two weeks.

CARDAMOM

This is one of my favorite spices. I love the depth it gives my baked goods. Leftover cardamom can be stored with the rest of your spices in an airtight container. It will keep for about a year. If you find yourself with leftover cardamom, try mixing it into a smoothie or bowl of oatmeal. It's great for spicing up a cup of tea, coffee, or even hot chocolate. Cardamom is often used in Indian cuisine, and I love to sprinkle it into any Indian stew I'm making. Also try making Chai-Spiced Snickerdoodles or Spiced Pumpkin Cheesecake with Gingersnap Crust.

VANILLA EXTRACT

Vanilla can be used for a wide variety of things. It lasts a long time, so you can keep it stored in your cabinet for years and years. Use a splash of vanilla with milk in your next cup of coffee for a vanilla latte. Vanilla is wonderful to add to any baked good. This includes cinnamon rolls, muffins, pancakes, waffles—you name it, vanilla will make it better. I'll even toss a drop of vanilla onto some fresh berries as a quick afternoon snack. Use vanilla in Earl Grey Cupcakes with Rosemary Honey Frosting or Classic Vanilla Bean Crème Brûlée).

ACTIVE DRY YEAST

Active dry yeast most commonly comes in packets of 2½ teaspoons. I usually tear open those packets, pour the contents of several into an airtight container, and then leave that container in my refrigerator for months and months. It's very convenient for small batch bread making. If you have leftover active dry yeast, try making Sesame Seed and Onion Bagels or Brioche Hamburger Buns. Yeast should always be stored in the refrigerator to keep it fresh.

THE BENEFITS OF WEIGHING INGREDIENTS

» **Precision:** Small batch baking, and baking in general, is all about precision. To produce consistent results in small batch baking, measure by weight. One cup of flour can weigh a slightly different amount each time you scoop it, so for the most accurate measure, weight is best.

» **Every gram counts:** Most scales provide gram and ounce measurements. The most accurate measurement is in grams, and when you're baking in small batches, every gram counts. Gram measurement is the most commonly used weight measurement among pastry professionals.

» **Time saver:** Rather than scooping and leveling several different cup measurements each time you bake, just adding an ingredient by scooping it into a bowl on a scale is much easier and saves time.

» **Liquid versus dry:** Liquid ingredients differ in weight from dry ingredients. One cup of milk is vastly different from 1 cup of flour, so weighing it by the gram is the easiest way to get the best result.

» **Baker's math:** Weight measurements make baker's math easy. If you decide to increase or decrease the yield, it's easier to do so when you are doing math by the gram rather than adding and subtracting fractions.

Baking 101

People can often get intimidated when it comes to baking, but really, it's not all that difficult! There are a few simple rules to follow to ensure that your baked goods are easy to prepare and come out tasting great. In this section, I'll go over some basic rules to follow. I will not only tell you what to do but also explain why you're doing it so you can better understand the baking process.

Read through the entire recipe before you start.

This is the most important rule in baking. It's important to understand everything you'll be doing and to determine whether you need to complete any steps before you start to bake. Baking is all about planning ahead.

Sift your dry ingredients.

Flour, granulated sugar, and powdered sugar are known to get clumpy, so sifting your ingredients before using them will ensure that your baked goods come out free of clumps. This simple rule is even more important in humid weather.

Allow your butter to come to room temperature.

This rule does not apply to pies and biscuits, but for mixing cookies, cakes, and especially frostings, room temperature butter is a must. Room temperature butter is much easier to mix than cold butter and can even be mixed by hand. Whenever a recipe calls for room temperature butter, just leave it out the night before you intend to bake. If you forget, an easy hack is simply to melt the butter whenever the recipe calls for room temperature butter. Cookies, cakes, muffins, and cupcakes can be made using this hack. However, frostings and breads must be made with room temperature butter.

Allow your cream cheese to come to room temperature.

Like butter, cream cheese is much easier to work with when it's at room temperature. The best cream cheese for baking comes in blocks, not tubs. They are completely wrapped, and the entire wrapped block of cream cheese should be left out the night before using. This is especially important for cheesecakes, as you want everything to mix easily for a creamy product.

Scoop out and level off dry ingredients in measuring cups.

If you are not using a kitchen scale, the best way to measure out dry ingredients is to scoop them into cups and level them off with a knife. This way, the ingredient is not packed in and not underfilled in any way. This is the easiest way to measure dry ingredients for the recipes in this book.

Know when to use nonstick baking spray and when to use parchment paper.

All the recipes will have clear guidance on when to use nonstick baking spray and when to use parchment paper. As a general rule, I use parchment whenever I'm baking something that will cover a large area, such as a cake or brownies. For pies and tarts, however, I simply use nonstick baking spray. Pie dough is less likely to stick to a baking pan than cake, due to the low sugar content.

Preheat the oven thoroughly before baking.

Certain baked goods need thorough heat to get the baking process started right. For instance, pie dough will just melt if the oven isn't preheated to the right temperature. It's always a good idea to have the oven preheated for at least 10 minutes before starting to bake.

STORING YOUR BAKED GOODS

Although the recipes in this book are for small batches, you may still end up with some leftovers. Here's what you can do to help keep them fresh for a few days.

BREADS AND BISCUITS

The best way to store leftover breads and biscuits is in a sealed bag. Store them at room temperature and they'll last about a week, or you can keep them for up to a month by freezing them.

MUFFINS, CAKES, AND CUPCAKES

These items keep best when covered and left in the refrigerator. They will last for up to a week.

COOKIES

The best way to store leftover cookies is in a sealed bag or airtight container. They will last for two weeks at room temperature or for up to two months if frozen.

BROWNIES AND BARS

Brownies and bars should be stored in a sealed bag or airtight container. They will last for a week at room temperature or for up to two months if frozen.

PIES AND TARTS

Leftover pies and tarts will last for up to a week covered in the refrigerator. I do not recommend freezing, as the quality will not hold up.

QUICHE

Quiche can be kept covered in the refrigerator for a week. Leftovers can be reheated in either a microwave for one minute or a 350°F preheated oven for 10 minutes. Freezing is not recommended.

CHEESECAKES

Leftovers should be covered and kept in the refrigerator. They will last for up to a week. They can be frozen for up to a month in an airtight container.

PUDDINGS

Pudding should be covered in plastic wrap and stored in the refrigerator. Leftover crème brûlée can be stored only if the sugar has not been caramelized on the top. Puddings will last up to a week. Freezing pudding is not recommended.

PASTRIES AND TURNOVERS

Leftovers can be kept in a sealed bag or an airtight container at room temperature. They will last up to four days. To reheat any of these items, you can microwave them for 30 seconds or heat in a 350°F oven for five to eight minutes.

ROSEMARY GOAT-CHEESE BISCUITS

CHAPTER 2
breads *and* biscuits

Honey Whole-Wheat Loaf

Hawaiian Potato Dinner Rolls

Brioche Hamburger Buns

Rosemary Goat-Cheese Biscuits

Chorizo Cheddar Cornmeal Biscuits

Parmesan, Rosemary, and Olive Focaccia

Mock Sourdough English Muffins

Sesame Seed and Onion Bagels

Honey Whole-Wheat Loaf

MAKES 1 LOAF **BAKING VESSEL:** LOAF PAN

Prep Time: 20 minutes, plus 2 hours to rise and 1 hour to cool /
Cook Time: 45 minutes

If you're into baking, as I am, you'll find that making your own bread can be very rewarding. It's a great feeling when you can make a nice loaf of bread in your own oven. In my opinion, it always tastes better, too. You can feel proud after making this loaf. Once you realize how easy the process actually is, you may never go back to buying store-bought bread again.

1¼ cups (283 grams) water

2¼ teaspoons (7 grams) active dry yeast

Nonstick baking spray

1⅓ cups (163 grams) all-purpose flour

2¼ cups (270 grams) whole-wheat flour

1½ teaspoons (9 grams) salt

¼ cup (85 grams) honey

2 tablespoons (28 grams) unsalted butter, at room temperature

1. In a small bowl, microwave the water in 30-second increments until it's lukewarm. Sprinkle the yeast over it and let it sit for 5 minutes to activate.

2. Spray a large bowl with nonstick baking spray.

3. Use a handheld electric mixer or a stand mixer fitted with the dough hook. Combine the all-purpose flour, whole-wheat flour, salt, and honey. Mix on low and add the yeast mixture. Add the butter last and mix on low for 5 minutes. Transfer the dough to the prepared bowl. Cover with plastic wrap and let rise in a warm area for 1 hour.

4. Spray a loaf pan with nonstick baking spray. Place the dough on a clean work surface. Roll it into a loaf shape and place it in the loaf pan. Loosely cover the pan with plastic wrap and let it rise for 1 hour.

5. Preheat the oven to 375°F.

6. Bake the loaf for 30 minutes. Reduce the temperature to 350°F and bake for an additional 15 minutes. The top should be evenly golden brown and the loaf should sound hollow when lightly tapped.

7. Cool the loaf on a wire rack at room temperature for 1 hour before slicing.

BAKING TIP: When working with dough, it's important not to overwork it. Handling the dough too much can deflate the yeast and leave your dough as dense as a brick. Be swift with your movements and work quickly to avoid overworking the dough.

Hawaiian Potato Dinner Rolls

MAKES 6 ROLLS **BAKING VESSEL:** LOAF PAN

Prep Time: 15 minutes, plus 3 hours to rise / **Cook Time:** 25 minutes

There's nothing better than a soft, pillowy dinner roll to go with a hearty meal. These rolls are sweetened with pineapple juice and are extra tender due to the addition of mashed potatoes. You can either boil a Russet potato and mash it or make up some mashed potatoes from a box.

⅓ cup (77 grams) pineapple juice

1 teaspoon (3 grams) active dry yeast

Nonstick baking spray

2 cups (240 grams) all-purpose flour

3 tablespoons (37 grams) granulated sugar

¾ teaspoon (4 grams) salt

½ cup (125 grams) mashed potatoes

1 egg

5 tablespoons (70 grams) unsalted butter, melted, divided

1. In a small bowl, microwave the pineapple juice for 10 to 20 seconds until it's lukewarm. Sprinkle the yeast over it and let it sit for 5 minutes to activate.

2. Spray a large bowl with nonstick baking spray.

3. Use a handheld electric mixer or a stand mixer fitted with the dough hook. In a large bowl, combine the flour, sugar, and salt. Mix on low until combined. Add the yeast mixture and then the mashed potatoes, egg, and 3 tablespoons of melted butter. Mix until the dough forms a ball, coming clean off the sides. Transfer the dough to the prepared bowl. Cover with plastic wrap and let rise in a warm area for 2 hours.

4. Spray a loaf pan with nonstick baking spray. Divide the dough into six equal pieces. You can either eyeball it or use a kitchen scale. Roll each piece into a ball and place it in the loaf pan. Cover the pan with plastic wrap and let rise for 1 hour.

5. Preheat the oven to 350°F.

6. Bake the rolls for 25 minutes, or until they're evenly browned. Remove from the oven and brush the tops with the remaining 2 tablespoons of melted butter.

INGREDIENT TIP: To give these buns that familiar yellow hue, add ¼ teaspoon of turmeric to the dough with the flour in step 2. It won't taste like the spice, but it'll enhance that "Hawaiian roll" aesthetic.

Brioche Hamburger Buns

MAKES 6 BUNS **BAKING VESSEL:** SHEET PAN

Prep Time: 20 minutes, plus 2 hours 15 minutes to rise / **Cook Time:** 20 minutes

In my opinion, good burgers start with good buns. I prefer a brioche bun because it's buttery and holds up well to a juicy burger. In this variation, I've included whole-wheat flour because I love the nutty taste it brings, but you can use all-purpose white flour if you prefer. These buns keep well frozen, so if the yield is too much, just freeze the extras in a sealed bag for up to a month.

¾ cup (255 grams) milk

1½ teaspoons (5 grams) active dry yeast

Nonstick baking spray

1½ cups (184 grams) all-purpose flour

¾ cup (106 grams) whole-wheat flour

1 teaspoon (6 grams) salt

1½ tablespoons (19 grams) granulated sugar

2 eggs, divided

1 egg yolk

2 tablespoons (28 grams) unsalted butter, at room temperature

1 tablespoon (15 grams) water

1. In a small bowl, microwave the milk for 30 seconds to 1 minute, until it's lukewarm. Sprinkle the yeast over it and let it sit for 5 minutes to activate.

2. Spray a large bowl with nonstick baking spray. Line a sheet pan with parchment paper.

3. Use a handheld electric mixer or a stand mixer fitted with the dough hook. In a large bowl, combine the all-purpose flour, whole-wheat flour, salt, and sugar. Turn the mixer on low and pour in the yeast mixture. Add 1 egg, then the yolk, and the butter last. Continue to mix on low until the dough is thoroughly mixed. It will be sticky. Transfer the dough to the prepared bowl. Cover with plastic wrap and let rise in a warm area until it has doubled in size, 1 to 1½ hours.

4. Divide the dough into six equal pieces. You can either eyeball it or use a kitchen scale. Roll each piece into a ball, and then press it down with the palm of your hand to flatten it a little. Place each bun on the lined sheet pan; space the buns about 4 inches apart. Cover the pan with plastic wrap and let rise again for 30 to 45 minutes, or until buns have doubled in size.

5. Preheat the oven to 375°F.

6. To make the egg wash, in a small bowl whisk the remaining egg and the water. Brush the egg wash over each roll. Bake the rolls for 15 to 20 minutes, or until they're evenly golden brown.

VARIATION TIP: To make a dairy-free version of these buns, substitute equal amounts of almond milk for the milk, and use olive oil instead of the butter.

Rosemary Goat-Cheese Biscuits

MAKES 6 BISCUITS **BAKING VESSEL:** SHEET PAN

Prep Time: 20 minutes / **Cook Time:** 15 minutes

There's nothing worse than a dry biscuit, and that's always on my mind when making them. This biscuit has loads of flavor, and the goat cheese gives it the moisture it needs. To create layers of flavor, I've included instructions on how to laminate the dough—basically, folding and rolling. Just like pie dough, you'll want to keep your biscuit dough very cold. This way the butter doesn't mix thoroughly into the dough, and when you bake it, those chunks of butter will create the flaky layers we all know and love.

2 cups (240 grams) all-purpose flour, plus more for rolling

½ cup (113 grams) goat cheese, at room temperature

2 teaspoons (9 grams) baking powder

½ teaspoon (3 grams) salt

6 tablespoons (85 grams) unsalted butter, cold, cubed

1 tablespoon (3 grams) chopped fresh rosemary

½ cup (113 grams) milk

1. Preheat the oven to 425°F. Line a sheet pan with parchment paper.

2. Use a handheld electric mixer or a stand mixer fitted with the dough hook. In a large bowl, combine the flour, goat cheese, baking powder, and salt. Mix to combine. Add the butter and rosemary. Mix on low for 1 minute. Continue to mix on low and drizzle in the milk. The dough should come together, but with some visible chunks of butter.

3. Roll out the dough on a floured work surface into a 12-by-16-inch rectangle. Fold one-third of the dough from the left side into the center. Then fold one-third from the right side over the other fold, creating a trifold. Roll out the dough again into a 12-by-16-inch rectangle and repeat the folds. Then do it one more time, for a total of three times. After the third set of folds, you should have a 6-by-8-inch rectangle. Cut it into six pieces by cutting it in half lengthwise and then cutting each half across in thirds.

4. Place the biscuits evenly on the lined sheet pan, spaced about 2 inches apart. Freeze the dough for 5 minutes.

5. Bake the biscuits for 15 minutes, or until they're puffed up and evenly browned. Serve immediately.

BAKING TIP: To save time, you can prepare these biscuits as directed and keep them in the freezer until you're ready to bake them. Since they'll be frozen when you put them in the oven, you'll need to add 2 to 3 minutes to the baking time.

Chorizo Cheddar Cornmeal Biscuits

MAKES 6 BISCUITS **BAKING VESSEL:** SHEET PAN

Prep Time: 15 minutes / **Cook Time:** 15 minutes

My husband's favorite food is chorizo, so I try to sneak it into the things I bake whenever possible. To create flaky layers, I've included directions on how to laminate the dough. Laminating is just a series of rolls and folds, and it makes a huge difference in the finished product. To avoid having scraps, I cut the dough into six equal pieces instead of punching it out with a cookie cutter. This dough comes together easiest in a stand mixer, but it can be made with some good old elbow grease as well.

1¼ cups (150 grams) all-purpose flour, plus more for rolling

½ cup (78 grams) cornmeal

2 teaspoons (9 grams) baking powder

1 tablespoon (13 grams) granulated sugar

½ teaspoon (3 grams) salt

5 tablespoons (75 grams) unsalted butter, cold, cubed

½ cup (55 grams) diced dried chorizo

¼ cup (58 grams) shredded cheddar cheese

½ cup (121 grams) buttermilk

1. Preheat the oven to 425°F. Line a sheet pan with parchment paper.

2. In the bowl of a stand mixer, combine the flour, cornmeal, baking powder, sugar, and salt. Mix to combine. Add the butter, chorizo, and cheddar. Mix on low for 1 minute. Continue to mix on low and drizzle in the buttermilk. The dough should come together with some visible chunks of butter. To mix the dough by hand, in a large bowl combine the flour, cornmeal, baking powder, sugar, and salt. Stir with a fork to combine. Add the butter, chorizo, and cheddar. Start working with a fork to cut the butter into the flour. Drizzle in the buttermilk, a little at a time, while working the dough with the fork. Continue until all the buttermilk is added and the dough begins to come together into a large mass with visible chunks of butter.

3. Roll out the dough on a floured work surface into a 12-by-16-inch rectangle. Fold one-third of the dough from the left side into the center. Then fold one-third from the right side over the other fold, creating a trifold. Roll out the dough again into a 12-by-16-inch rectangle and repeat the folds. Then do it one more time, for a total of three times. After the third set of folds, you should have a 6-by-8-inch rectangle. Cut it into six pieces by cutting it in half lengthwise and then cutting each half across in thirds.

4. Place the biscuits evenly on the lined sheet pan, spaced about 2 inches apart. Freeze the dough for 5 minutes.

5. Bake the biscuits for 15 minutes, or until they're puffed up and evenly browned. Serve immediately.

INGREDIENT TIP: If you can't find dried chorizo, 6 ounces of Mexican chorizo will do. Cook it in a skillet over medium heat to render out the fat. Drain and cool the chorizo before adding it to the biscuit dough.

Parmesan, Rosemary, and Olive Focaccia

MAKES 6 SLICES **BAKING VESSEL:** LOAF PAN

Prep Time: 10 minutes, plus 1 hour 45 minutes to rise / **Cook Time:** 20 minutes

I took a trip to Italy a few years ago and fell in love with focaccia. It amazes me how just a few simple ingredients—flour, water, olive oil, yeast, and salt—can make such a delicious product. What amazed me more was figuring out how easy it was to actually make. You can make this all in one bowl with a single spatula or just your hands. Feel free to change the flavors to suit your preferences. Sun-dried tomatoes, jalapeño peppers, and marinated artichokes are all great additions.

½ cup (113 grams) water

1 teaspoon (3 grams) active dry yeast

1¼ cups (154 grams) all-purpose flour

5 tablespoons (66 grams) olive oil, divided

½ teaspoon (3 grams) salt

1 tablespoon (3 grams) chopped fresh rosemary

¼ cup (45 grams) pitted and sliced black olives

Nonstick baking spray

2 tablespoons (11 grams) shredded Parmesan cheese

1. In a small bowl, microwave the water for 20 to 30 seconds until it's lukewarm. Sprinkle the yeast over it and let it sit for 5 minutes to activate.

2. In a medium bowl, combine the flour, 3 tablespoons of oil, salt, and the yeast mixture. Mix with a spatula until all the dry bits have been mixed in. Add the rosemary and olives. The dough will be very loose and wet.

3. In a large bowl, pour 1 tablespoon of oil and spread it around until the bowl is well greased. Put the dough in the bowl and then flip it so all the dough is coated in oil. Cover the bowl with plastic wrap and let rise for 30 minutes. Then uncover the dough. Wet your hands, take one side of the dough, and fold it over the center. Take the other side of the dough and fold it over the center. Take the top side of the dough and pull it down to the bottom. Then take the bottom side of the dough and pull it over the top. Cover with plastic wrap and let it rise for 30 minutes more.

4. Spray a loaf pan thoroughly with nonstick baking spray. Place the dough in the pan, stretching it with your fingers to fill the pan. Poke indents into the top of the dough. Sprinkle the remaining 1 tablespoon of oil and the Parmesan over the top. Cover with plastic wrap and let it rise for 45 minutes.

5. Preheat the oven to 425°F.

6. Bake the focaccia for 20 minutes, or until it's evenly browned. Cool on a wire rack; then slice into six pieces.

BAKING TIP: Working this dough with your hands can get a little messy. To avoid sticking, wet your hands with warm water before handling it.

Mock Sourdough English Muffins

MAKES 6 MUFFINS **BAKING VESSELS:** SHEET PAN, LARGE SKILLET

Prep Time: 20 minutes, plus overnight to ferment and 2 hours 30 minutes to rise / **Cook Time:** 10 minutes

I love a good English muffin! During the COVID-19 quarantine, I'd make myself a batch each week because bread was so scarce in the grocery stores. I call this a mock sourdough English muffin because instead of using sourdough culture, I've included a poolish, which is a pre-ferment, to give this muffin its sour note. You should start the poolish the night before you want to make these muffins to give the flavors time to develop.

FOR THE POOLISH

¼ cup (57 grams) water

¼ teaspoon (0.7 grams) active dry yeast

⅓ cup (43 grams) all-purpose flour

FOR THE DOUGH

½ cup (113 grams) milk

¼ teaspoon (0.7 grams) active dry yeast

Nonstick baking spray

1 tablespoon (12 grams) granulated sugar

1½ cups (184 grams) all-purpose flour

½ teaspoon (3 grams) salt

Poolish

1 egg yolk

Cornmeal, for sprinkling

TO MAKE THE POOLISH

1. In a small bowl, microwave the water for 20 seconds until it's lukewarm. Sprinkle the yeast over it and let it sit for 5 minutes to activate.

2. Whisk in the flour. Cover the bowl with plastic wrap and let it ferment at room temperature for 8 hours or overnight.

TO MAKE THE DOUGH

3. In a small bowl, microwave the milk for 20 seconds to 1 minute until it's lukewarm. Sprinkle the yeast over it and let it sit for 5 minutes to activate.

4. Spray a large bowl with nonstick baking spray.

5. Use a handheld electric mixer or a stand mixer fitted with the dough hook. In a large bowl, combine the sugar, flour, and salt and mix on low. Add the poolish, yeast mixture, and egg yolk. Mix until the dough is smooth; it will be loose and tacky.

6. Put the dough in the prepared bowl. Cover with plastic wrap and let it rise at room temperature for 2 hours, or until it has doubled in size.

7. Line a sheet pan with parchment paper and sprinkle it with an even layer of cornmeal.

8. Divide the dough into six equal pieces. You can either eyeball it or use a kitchen scale. Roll each piece into a ball, and then flatten it with the palm of your hand. Place each piece of dough on the sheet pan. Cover the pan loosely with plastic wrap and let rise for 30 minutes.

9. Heat a large skillet on medium-low heat for 5 minutes. Once heated, spray it with nonstick baking spray. Use a flat spatula to lift a couple of the English muffins into the pan; then reduce the heat to low. Cook the English muffins for 5 minutes on each side, or until each side has evenly browned. Repeat with the remaining muffins.

10. Serve immediately, or store in an airtight container for up to 5 days.

VARIATION TIP: Whole-wheat English muffins are great, too. Use ¾ cup (92 grams) of whole-wheat flour and ¾ cup (92 grams) of all-purpose flour when you prepare the dough, and proceed as directed.

Sesame Seed and Onion Bagels

MAKES 6 BAGELS **BAKING VESSELS:** LARGE POT, SHEET PAN

Prep Time: 20 minutes, plus 2 hours 30 minutes to rise / **Cook Time:** 20 minutes

Bagels are great for so many things. Cream cheese, vegetable spreads, and eggs are all complemented by a good bagel. This is a fun recipe to make with kids. Allowing them to carefully slip the bagel into the water with a large slotted spoon, sprinkle on the toppings, and then eat the final result is a great way to introduce them to cooking.

1 cup (226 grams) water

¾ teaspoon (2 grams) active dry yeast

Nonstick baking spray

3 cups (360 grams) all-purpose flour

1 tablespoon (12 grams) packed light brown sugar

1 teaspoon (6 grams) salt

1 egg white

1 tablespoon (7 grams) dried onion flakes

1 tablespoon (9 grams) sesame seeds

1. In a small bowl, microwave the water for 30 to 60 seconds until it's lukewarm. Sprinkle the yeast over it and let it sit for 5 minutes to activate.

2. Spray a large bowl with nonstick baking spray. Line a sheet pan with parchment paper.

3. Use a handheld electric mixer or a stand mixer fitted with the dough hook. In a large bowl, combine the flour, brown sugar, and salt. Add the yeast mixture and mix on low until the dough has formed a ball and comes clean off the sides.

4. Put the dough in the prepared bowl. Cover with plastic wrap and let rise in a warm area for 1 to 1½ hours, or until it has doubled in size.

5. Divide the dough into six equal pieces. You can either eyeball it or use a kitchen scale. Roll each piece into a ball, and then flatten it with the palm of your hand. Poke a hole into the center of each ball and stretch the hole out to 2 inches wide. Place each bagel on the lined sheet pan. Loosely cover the pan with plastic wrap and let bagels rise for 1 hour or up to 24 hours in the refrigerator.

6. Preheat the oven to 450°F.

7. In a large pot, bring 3 quarts of water to a boil. Put the egg white in a small bowl and set aside.

8. Carefully drop 2 bagels into the boiling water. Boil for 1 minute, flip, and then boil for 1 minute more. Use a large slotted spoon to take the bagels out of the water and place them back on the sheet pan. Let the bagels air dry for 1 minute; then brush them with egg white and top with onion flakes and sesame seeds. Repeat with the remaining bagels.

9. Bake the bagels for 15 minutes, or until they're evenly browned.

VARIATION TIP: For a sweeter bagel, try cinnamon sugar as a topping instead. Combine 2 tablespoons (25 grams) of sugar and ½ teaspoon (1 gram) of cinnamon in a small bowl. When you take the bagel out of the boiling water, let it air dry for 1 minute; then brush it with egg white and sprinkle on the cinnamon sugar.

LEMON MERINGUE CUPCAKES

CHAPTER 3
muffins *and* cupcakes

Lemon Poppy Seed Sour Cream Muffins

Pumpkin Walnut Muffins

Banana Blueberry Muffins

Peach Streusel Muffins

Lemon Meringue Cupcakes

Classic Yellow Cupcakes with Chocolate Fudge Frosting

Chocolate Cupcakes with Peanut-Butter Pretzel Frosting

Strawberry Cupcakes with White Chocolate Cream Cheese Frosting

Earl Grey Cupcakes with Rosemary-Honey Frosting

Lemon Poppy Seed Sour Cream Muffins

MAKES 6 MUFFINS **BAKING VESSEL:** MUFFIN TIN

Prep Time: 20 minutes / **Cook Time:** 20 minutes

This delicate muffin is light and tender, and the sour cream delivers extra moistness. The hint of pretty poppy seeds gives this breakfast pastry extra flavor. Personally, I love this muffin with a hot cup of chamomile tea, but Earl Grey or coffee will do nicely, too.

3 tablespoons (42 grams) unsalted butter, melted

⅓ cup (43 grams) granulated sugar

1 egg white

¾ cup plus 2 tablespoons (112 grams) all-purpose flour

¼ teaspoon (1 gram) baking soda

½ teaspoon (2 grams) baking powder

⅛ teaspoon salt

½ cup (123 grams) sour cream

1 tablespoon (6 grams) lemon zest

2 tablespoons (28 grams) lemon juice

1 tablespoon (9 grams) poppy seeds

1. Preheat the oven to 375°F. Line six cups of a muffin tin with cupcake liners.

2. In a medium bowl, whisk together the melted butter and sugar. Add the egg white and whisk until smooth. Use a rubber spatula to fold in the flour, baking soda, baking powder, and salt. Stir in the sour cream, lemon zest, lemon juice, and poppy seeds.

3. Divide the batter evenly among the six cups, filling them almost all the way to the top. Bake the muffins for 20 minutes. Let cool in the pan for 10 minutes, and then serve.

BAKING TIP: For freshly baked muffins in the morning, make the batter and fill the muffin tin the night before. Keep it in the refrigerator overnight. In the morning, just pop the whole thing in the preheated oven.

Pumpkin Walnut Muffins

MAKES 6 MUFFINS **BAKING VESSEL:** MUFFIN TIN

Prep Time: 20 minutes / **Cook Time:** 25 minutes

Cool weather and pumpkins signal one of my favorite times of the year: fall. I love when the seasons change and I get to play with an entirely new set of flavors—pumpkin being one of the best pastry flavors out there. These muffins are super easy to make. For even more convenience, make the batter up to three days ahead, store it in the refrigerator, and bake them without fuss in the morning.

¼ cup (55 grams) canola oil

¾ cup (184 grams) pumpkin puree

¼ cup (50 grams) packed light brown sugar

¼ cup (50 grams) granulated sugar

1 egg

1 cup (125 grams) all-purpose flour

½ teaspoon (2 grams) baking soda

¼ teaspoon (1.5 grams) salt

1 teaspoon (2 grams) ground cinnamon

½ teaspoon (1 gram) ground ginger

½ cup (50 grams) chopped walnuts

1. Preheat the oven to 375°F. Line six cups of a muffin tin with cupcake liners.

2. In a medium bowl, whisk together the oil, pumpkin puree, brown sugar, and granulated sugar. Add the egg and whisk until smooth. Add the flour, baking soda, salt, cinnamon, and ginger, and fold in with a spatula until smooth. Fold in the walnuts last. Divide the batter evenly among the six cups, filling them almost all the way to the top.

3. Bake the muffins for 22 to 25 minutes, or until a toothpick inserted comes out clean. Let cool in the pan for 10 minutes, and then serve.

VARIATION TIP: If pumpkin isn't your thing, try making apple walnut muffins instead. Substitute the same amount of applesauce for the pumpkin puree and prepare as directed.

Banana Blueberry Muffins

MAKES *6 MUFFINS* **BAKING VESSEL:** *MUFFIN TIN*

Prep Time: 20 minutes / **Cook Time:** 30 minutes

The only way to improve on a classic blueberry muffin is by adding banana. In fact, this flavor combination is one of my favorites. Double this recipe and bake it in a loaf pan for blueberry banana bread.

⅓ cup (67 grams) blueberries

1 tablespoon (14 grams) all-purpose flour, plus 1 cup (120 grams)

¼ cup (57 grams) unsalted butter, at room temperature

¼ cup (50 grams) granulated sugar

¼ cup (50 grams) packed light brown sugar

1 egg white

¾ cup (225 grams) mashed banana

½ teaspoon (2 grams) baking soda

¼ teaspoon (1.5 grams) salt

1. Preheat the oven to 375°F. Line six cups of a muffin tin with cupcake liners.

2. In a small bowl, toss the blueberries with 1 tablespoon of flour to coat evenly.

3. Using a stand mixer fitted with the paddle attachment or a handheld electric mixer, mix the butter, granulated sugar, and brown sugar together in a large bowl. Add the egg white and then the mashed banana. Add the remaining 1 cup of flour, baking soda, and salt, and mix until the batter is smooth. Fold in the floured blueberries last. Divide the batter evenly among the six cups, filling them nearly to the top.

4. Bake the muffins for 25 to 28 minutes, or until a toothpick inserted comes out clean. Let cool in the pan for 10 minutes, and then serve.

VARIATION TIP: Swap out the blueberries for raspberries if you'd like. Use the same amount, and make sure you toss them in flour before adding them to the batter so they don't all sink to the bottom.

Peach Streusel Muffins

MAKES 6 MUFFINS **BAKING VESSEL:** MUFFIN TIN

Prep Time: 25 minutes / **Cook Time:** 25 minutes

I grew up with a peach tree in my backyard and it's one of my favorite flavors. Plums, apricots, or nectarines will also work very well here.

FOR THE STREUSEL

1 tablespoon (14 grams) unsalted butter, melted

2 tablespoons (16 grams) all-purpose flour

2 tablespoons (19 grams) rolled oats

⅛ teaspoon cinnamon

1 tablespoon (12 grams) packed light brown sugar

FOR THE MUFFINS

¼ cup (57 grams) unsalted butter, melted

¼ cup (50 grams) granulated sugar

¼ cup (50 grams) packed light brown sugar

1 egg white

¼ teaspoon (1.5 grams) salt

1 cup (125 grams) all-purpose flour

⅛ teaspoon cinnamon

½ teaspoon (2 grams) baking soda

¾ cup peeled and diced peaches (about 1 large peach)

TO MAKE THE STREUSEL

1. In a small bowl, combine the butter, flour, oats, cinnamon, and brown sugar. Set aside.

TO MAKE THE MUFFINS

2. Preheat the oven to 375°F. Line six cups of a muffin tin with cupcake liners.

3. In a medium bowl, whisk together the butter, granulated sugar, and brown sugar. Add the egg white and whisk until smooth. Use a rubber spatula to fold in the salt, flour, cinnamon, and baking soda. Fold in the peaches last.

4. Divide the batter evenly among the six cups, filling them almost all the way to the top. Sprinkle the streusel over the tops of the muffins. Bake the muffins for 25 minutes. Let cool in the pan for 10 minutes, and then serve.

INGREDIENT TIP: An easy way to peel peaches is to drop each peach in boiling water for 30 seconds to 1 minute. Immediately transfer it to a bowl filled with ice water to cool down. The skin should then slide right off.

Lemon Meringue Cupcakes

MAKES 6 CUPCAKES **BAKING VESSEL:** MUFFIN TIN

Prep Time: 20 minutes, plus 30 minutes to cool / **Cook Time:** 15 minutes

If you aren't a fan of lemon desserts, then you don't know what you're missing. Lemon and sugar go together so well! In this cupcake, I wanted to recreate the flavors of lemon meringue pie. The cake is lighter than air and is packed with lemon flavor. The topping is an easy meringue, making this cupcake a perfect sweet and tart treat.

⅓ **cup (80 grams) canola oil**

¾ **cup (150 grams) granulated sugar, divided**

3 egg whites, divided

½ **cup plus 2 tablespoons (80 grams) all-purpose flour**

¾ **teaspoon (3 grams) baking powder**

⅛ **teaspoon salt**

Zest of 1 lemon

4 tablespoons (57 grams) lemon juice

½ **teaspoon (3 grams) vanilla extract**

1. Preheat the oven to 375°F. Line six cups of a muffin tin with cupcake liners.

2. In a medium bowl, whisk together the oil and ½ cup (100 grams) of sugar. Add 1 egg white and whisk to combine. Add the flour, baking powder, and salt, and fold in with a spatula. Add the lemon zest and lemon juice; then stir with a spatula until the batter is smooth. Divide the batter evenly among the six cups, filling them about three-quarters of the way up.

3. Bake for 15 to 18 minutes, or until a toothpick inserted comes out clean. Transfer to a wire rack and cool completely to room temperature, about 30 minutes.

4. To make the meringue, use a stand mixer fitted with the whisk attachment, or a handheld electric mixer. Add the remaining 2 egg whites to a large bowl. Turn the mixer on and slowly add the remaining ¼ cup (50 grams) of sugar. Whip until it starts to form stiff peaks. Add the vanilla last. Transfer the meringue to a piping bag or a zip-top bag with the bottom corner snipped off.

5. Pipe the meringue onto the cupcakes. Use a kitchen blowtorch to brown the meringue topping. Serve immediately.

BAKING TIP: If you don't have a kitchen blowtorch, you can easily brown the meringue under a broiler. Heat the broiler on high and place the cupcakes about 2 inches from the broiling element. Watch carefully and remove them after about 2 minutes, or when the meringue is browned to your liking.

Classic Yellow Cupcakes with Chocolate Fudge Frosting

MAKES 6 CUPCAKES **BAKING VESSEL:** MUFFIN TIN

Prep Time: 20 minutes, plus 30 minutes to cool / **Cook Time:** 20 minutes

My mom's favorite baked dessert is a classic yellow cupcake with chocolate fudge frosting. It's simple, delicious, and rich. Using only the egg yolks makes the cake more yellow—the chocolate fudge frosting being the perfect contrast. If you want a richer frosting, try using milk chocolate instead of semisweet chocolate chips. Milk chocolate is creamier, and top-quality chocolate makes a big difference.

FOR THE CUPCAKES

½ cup (64 grams) all-purpose flour

¼ teaspoon (1 gram) baking powder

¼ teaspoon (1 gram) baking soda

⅛ teaspoon salt

2 tablespoons (28 grams) unsalted butter, melted

¼ cup (50 grams) granulated sugar

2 egg yolks

2 tablespoons (30 grams) sour cream

1 tablespoon (14 grams) milk

FOR THE FROSTING

¼ cup (40 grams) semisweet chocolate chips

10 tablespoons (141 grams) unsalted butter, at room temperature

¼ cup (25 grams) unsweetened cocoa powder

½ cup (50 grams) powdered sugar, sifted

Pinch salt

½ teaspoon (3 grams) vanilla extract

TO MAKE THE CUPCAKES

1. Preheat the oven to 375°F. Line six cups of a muffin tin with cupcake liners.

2. In a medium bowl, combine the flour, baking powder, baking soda, and salt. Set aside.

3. In a large bowl, whisk together the melted butter and sugar. Add the egg yolks to the sugar mixture and mix to combine. Then add the dry ingredients, sour cream, and finally the milk. Mix until the batter is very smooth.

4. Divide the batter evenly among the six cups, filling them about three-quarters of the way up. Bake the cupcakes for 12 minutes. Transfer to a wire rack and cool completely to room temperature, about 30 minutes.

TO MAKE THE FROSTING

5. Put the chocolate in a microwave-safe bowl and heat it in the microwave in 30-second increments until it's fully melted.

6. In a stand mixer fitted with the paddle attachment or a handheld electric mixer and a large bowl, combine the melted chocolate and butter. Mix until it's smooth, then add the cocoa powder, powdered sugar, salt, and vanilla. Keep mixing until the frosting is smooth. Scrape down the sides as needed. Transfer the frosting to a piping bag fitted with a piping tip or a zip-top bag with a bottom corner snipped off.

7. Pipe the frosting onto the cupcakes and serve immediately.

VARIATION TIP: Make a gluten-free version of this cupcake by substituting a gluten-free flour. I prefer to use the kind that already has xanthan gum in the mix, as it helps with binding.

Chocolate Cupcakes with Peanut-Butter Pretzel Frosting

MAKES 6 CUPCAKES **BAKING VESSEL:** MUFFIN TIN

Prep Time: 20 minutes, plus 30 minutes to cool / **Cook Time:** 20 minutes

I love everything chocolate. Sometimes a little chocolate cupcake is all you need to shake off a bad day. This sweet and salty cupcake is perfect for any palette. The crushed pretzels give the perfect salty contrast to an otherwise sweet treat. If you want to try a variation, salty potato chips would also work well! You never knew you needed these cupcakes in your life until now.

FOR THE CUPCAKES

⅓ cup (43 grams) all-purpose flour

¼ cup (25 grams) unsweetened cocoa powder

¼ teaspoon (1 gram) baking soda

¼ teaspoon (1.5 grams) salt

2 tablespoons (28 grams) canola oil

¼ cup (50 grams) packed light brown sugar

¼ cup (50 grams) granulated sugar

1 egg

¼ cup (60 grams) buttermilk

FOR THE FROSTING

½ cup (120 grams) peanut butter

½ cup (113 grams) unsalted butter, at room temperature

½ cup (50 grams) powdered sugar, sifted

⅛ teaspoon salt

½ teaspoon (3 grams) vanilla extract

½ cup (30 grams) crushed pretzels

TO MAKE THE CUPCAKES

1. Preheat the oven to 375°F. Line six cups of a muffin tin with cupcake liners.

2. In a medium bowl, combine the flour, cocoa powder, baking soda, and salt. Set aside.

3. In a large bowl, whisk together the oil, brown sugar, and granulated sugar. Add the egg to the sugar mixture and mix to combine. Then add the dry ingredients. Add the buttermilk last. Mix the batter until it's smooth.

4. Divide the batter evenly among the six cups, filling them about halfway up. Bake the cupcakes for 18 minutes. Transfer to a wire rack and cool completely to room temperature, about 30 minutes.

TO MAKE THE FROSTING

5. In a stand mixer fitted with the paddle attachment or a handheld electric mixer and a large bowl, combine the peanut butter and butter. Add the powdered sugar, salt, and vanilla, and mix until very smooth. Transfer the frosting to a piping bag fitted with a piping tip or a zip-top bag with a bottom corner snipped off.

6. Pipe the frosting onto the cupcakes, and garnish with crushed pretzels. Serve immediately.

INGREDIENT TIP: If you don't have buttermilk, you can substitute 3 tablespoons of milk and 1 tablespoon of lemon juice. Easy swap!

Strawberry Cupcakes with White Chocolate Cream Cheese Frosting

MAKES 6 CUPCAKES **BAKING VESSEL:** MUFFIN TIN

Prep Time: 20 minutes, plus 30 minutes to cool / **Cook Time:** 25 minutes

My favorite cake is strawberry—the boxed version, if you can believe it! I'm a fiend for anything strawberry. I wanted to recreate that cake for this book in an easy way using fresh berries. I love the flavor that fresh berries bring to the table—not an extract, but real strawberries. On its own, this cake comes out light pink. If you'd like to pump up the color a little, add one or two drops of red food coloring into the batter and mix just before baking.

FOR THE CUPCAKES

½ cup (100 grams) strawberries, hulled (5 to 6 strawberries)

2 tablespoons (28 grams) milk

¼ cup (60 grams) canola oil

½ cup (100 grams) granulated sugar

1 egg white

¾ cup (96 grams) all-purpose flour

½ teaspoon (2 grams) baking powder

⅛ teaspoon salt

FOR THE FROSTING

¼ cup (40 grams) white chocolate chips

¾ cup (90 grams) cream cheese, at room temperature

6 tablespoon (85 grams) unsalted butter, at room temperature

½ cup (50 grams) powdered sugar, sifted

TO MAKE THE CUPCAKES

1. Preheat the oven to 375°F. Line six cups of a muffin tin with cupcake liners.

2. In a small bowl, combine the strawberries, milk, and oil. Mash with a fork until the strawberries have slightly blended into the liquid or combine them in a blender and blend until smooth.

3. In a medium bowl, add the strawberry mixture and sugar and whisk until smooth. Whisk in the egg white. Use a rubber spatula to fold in the flour, baking powder, and salt. Mix until everything is combined.

4. Divide the batter evenly among the six cups, filling them about three-quarters of the way up. Bake the cupcakes for 20 to 25 minutes, or until a toothpick inserted comes out clean. Transfer to a wire rack and cool completely to room temperature, about 30 minutes.

TO MAKE THE FROSTING

5. Put the white chocolate in a microwave-safe bowl and heat it in the microwave in 30-second increments until it's fully melted.

6. In a stand mixer fitted with the paddle attachment or a handheld electric mixer and a large bowl, mix the cream cheese and butter together. Add the powdered sugar and melted chocolate. Mix until it's very smooth. Transfer the frosting to a piping bag fitted with a piping tip or a zip-top bag with a bottom corner snipped off.

7. Pipe the frosting onto the cupcakes and serve immediately.

INGREDIENT TIP: If you are using frozen strawberries, make sure you completely thaw them before preparing this recipe.

Earl Grey Cupcakes with Rosemary-Honey Frosting

MAKES 6 CUPCAKES **BAKING VESSEL:** MUFFIN TIN

Prep Time: 20 minutes, plus 30 minutes to cool / **Cook Time:** 20 minutes

This flavor combination is truly unique and has quickly become one of my favorites. The Earl Grey flavor permeates the cake so thoroughly that you'll soon wonder why you've never thought of baking with Earl Grey tea before. Rosemary is then infused with honey to make the ultimate buttercream topping for an already amazing cupcake. You might want to eat these all yourself, and I wouldn't blame you!

FOR THE CUPCAKES

⅓ cup (80 grams) canola oil

½ cup (100 grams) granulated sugar

1 egg white

½ cup (64 grams) all-purpose flour

¾ teaspoon (3 grams) baking powder

⅛ teaspoon salt

¼ cup (85 grams) milk

Leaves from 1 Earl Grey teabag or 2 teaspoons loose tea

FOR THE FROSTING

¼ cup (85 grams) honey

1 sprig fresh rosemary

6 tablespoon (85 grams) unsalted butter, at room temperature

¾ cup (75 grams) powdered sugar, sifted

2 tablespoons (28 grams) milk

TO MAKE THE CUPCAKES

1. Preheat the oven to 375°F. Line six cups of a muffin tin with cupcake liners.

2. In a large bowl, whisk together the oil and sugar. Add the egg white and whisk to combine. Add the flour, baking powder, and salt, and fold in with a spatula. Add the milk and tea leaves. Stir with a spatula until the batter is smooth.

3. Divide the batter evenly among the six cups, filling them about three-quarters of the way up. Bake for 15 to 18 minutes, or until a toothpick inserted comes out clean. Transfer to a wire rack and cool completely to room temperature, about 30 minutes, while you make the frosting.

TO MAKE THE FROSTING

4. In a small saucepan, heat the honey and rosemary over low heat. Do not boil. When the honey is hot, turn the heat off and let the rosemary infuse for 10 minutes. Then remove the rosemary sprig and transfer the honey to a small bowl and cool in the refrigerator for 10 minutes.

5. In a stand mixer fitted with the paddle attachment or a handheld electric mixer and a large bowl, combine the butter and powdered sugar. Mix until smooth, scraping the sides down as needed. Add the honey and then the milk, and mix until smooth. Transfer the frosting to a piping bag fitted with a piping tip or a zip-top bag with a bottom corner snipped off.

6. Pipe the frosting onto the cupcakes and serve immediately.

VARIATION TIP: Be sure to use a good-quality tea. Try switching the Earl Grey out for a bag of chamomile tea. They are both great teas to pair with dessert, so why not put them *in* a dessert?

MILLIONAIRE SHORTBREAD BARS WITH CARAMEL AND CHOCOLATE GANACHE

CHAPTER 4
cookies, brownies, *and* bars

Almond-Butter Cookies

Buttery Shortbread

Brown Butter Chocolate Chip Cookies with Sea Salt

Chai-Spiced Snickerdoodles

Double Chocolate Chunk Brownies

Peanut Butter Blondies

Carrot Cake Bars with Cream Cheese Swirl

Raspberry Oatmeal Almond Crumb Bars

Millionaire Shortbread Bars with Caramel and Chocolate Ganache

Almond-Butter Cookies

MAKES 12 COOKIES **BAKING VESSEL:** 2 SHEET PANS

Prep Time: 10 minutes, plus 30 minutes to cool / **Cook Time:** 10 minutes

Nut-butter cookies are a must-have in my house. My husband loves peanut butter, but I prefer almond butter, which is what's in this recipe. You can switch up the almond butter for an equal amount of any other nut butter, though, including peanut. Cashew, hazelnut, and sunflower butters are all great options.

6 tablespoons (85 grams) almond butter

6 tablespoons (85 grams) unsalted butter

¼ cup (50 grams) packed light brown sugar

2 tablespoons (25 grams) granulated sugar

1 egg yolk

¾ cup plus 2 tablespoons (112 grams) all-purpose flour

½ teaspoon (2 grams) baking soda

¼ teaspoon (1 gram) baking powder

½ teaspoon (3 grams) salt

1 tablespoon (15 grams) milk

1. Preheat the oven to 350°F. Line two sheet pans with parchment paper.

2. In a stand mixer fitted with the paddle attachment or with a handheld electric mixer and a large bowl, combine the almond butter, butter, brown sugar, and granulated sugar. Mix to combine. Add the egg yolk, flour, baking soda, baking powder, and salt. Add the milk last. Mix until the batter is smooth.

3. Use a soup spoon to scoop out 12 heaping tablespoons of cookie dough, spaced out 3 inches apart on the pans. Bake for 10 minutes.

4. Transfer the cookies to a wire rack to cool at room temperature for 30 minutes. Store in an airtight container.

INGREDIENT TIP: Some nut butters will separate if they haven't been used in a while. Make sure you stir the nut butter before using it.

Buttery Shortbread

MAKES 12 COOKIES **BAKING VESSEL:** 8-INCH-SQUARE BAKING PAN

Prep Time: 10 minutes, plus 1 hour 10 minutes to cool / **Cook Time:** 45 minutes

Shortbread cookies are perfectly buttery and tender and the best accompaniment to coffee and tea. This recipe couldn't be easier to make. After the dough comes together, you simply press it into the baking pan, score, and bake. Voilà!

Nonstick baking spray

1 cup (227 grams) unsalted butter, at room temperature

¾ cup (75 grams) powdered sugar

½ teaspoon (3 grams) salt

½ teaspoon (3 grams) vanilla extract

2 cups (240 grams) all-purpose flour

1. Preheat the oven to 300°F. Lightly spray a baking pan with nonstick baking spray. Then line it with a piece of parchment paper large enough to go 2 inches up the sides.

2. In a stand mixer fitted with the paddle attachment or a handheld electric mixer and a large bowl, cream the butter and powdered sugar together. Add the salt, vanilla, and then flour. The mixture should be crumbly. Press the dough into the baking pan in an even layer. Put the pan in the freezer for 5 minutes.

3. Before baking, score the top of the dough with a small, sharp knife. Stick the knife into the dough about halfway deep and cut a line right down the center. Turn the pan 45 degrees and run the knife right down the center again. Now you have four square sections. With the pan held in the same position, score the left side (top and bottom) into thirds and the right side into thirds, creating 12 rectangular cookies.

4. Bake the shortbread for 45 minutes, or until the edges are lightly golden brown. Remove it from the oven and immediately run the knife along where it was scored, separating the cookies. Let the shortbread cool in the pan for 10 minutes, then use the parchment to lift it up from the sides and cool on a wire rack for 1 hour. Store in an airtight container.

INGREDIENT TIP: If you only have salted butter in your refrigerator, there's no need to go out and buy unsalted butter; you can still use it for this recipe. Omit the salt and use the same amount of butter listed.

Brown Butter Chocolate Chip Cookies with Sea Salt

MAKES 12 COOKIES **BAKING VESSEL:** 2 SHEET PANS

Prep Time: 35 minutes / **Cook Time:** 10 minutes

Although I am a pastry chef, sometimes all I crave is a chocolate chip cookie. What is better than this classic? A chocolate chip cookie made with brown butter! The caramel-nutty notes of brown butter combined with just a hint of salt will keep you going back bite after bite. Look for high-quality, all-natural sea salt flakes.

6 tablespoons (85 grams) unsalted butter, cold

⅓ cup (65 grams) packed light brown sugar

⅓ cup (43 grams) granulated sugar

½ teaspoon (3 grams) salt

1 egg

½ teaspoon vanilla

1 cup (120 grams) all-purpose flour

¼ teaspoon (1 gram) baking powder

½ cup (80 grams) semisweet chocolate chips

¼ teaspoon (1.5 grams) sea salt flakes

1. Preheat the oven to 350°F. Line two sheet pans with parchment paper.

2. Heat the butter in a small saucepan on medium-high heat. Melt it completely, and then allow the milk solids to caramelize. When the butter starts to brown, pull the saucepan from the heat—all in all, this should take 3 to 5 minutes. Let it cool for 5 minutes.

3. In a medium bowl, use a rubber spatula to combine the brown sugar, granulated sugar, and salt. Drizzle in the cooled brown butter and mix. Add the egg, vanilla, flour, and baking powder, and mix to combine. Add the chocolate chips last.

4. Use a soup spoon to scoop the cookie dough onto the sheet pans, leaving 3 inches between cookies. Freeze the cookies on the sheet tray for 10 minutes, and then bake for 10 minutes.

5. Remove the cookies from the oven, lightly sprinkle with sea salt flakes, and transfer them to a wire rack to cool completely. Store in an airtight container.

BAKING TIP: I like to keep a stash of cookie dough in my freezer for when a craving hits. Just make the dough as directed and then scoop and freeze it on a sheet pan. Once frozen, put the scoops of dough in plastic zip-top freezer bags, and when you want a cookie, bake from frozen at 350°F for 10 minutes.

Chai-Spiced Snickerdoodles

MAKES 12 COOKIES **BAKING VESSEL:** 2 SHEET PANS

Prep Time: 10 minutes, plus 20 minutes to chill and 30 minutes to cool / **Cook Time:** 10 minutes

FOR THE COOKIES

4 tablespoons (56 grams) unsalted butter, melted

2 tablespoons (28 grams) packed light brown sugar

½ cup (100 grams) granulated sugar

1 egg

½ teaspoon (3 grams) vanilla extract

¼ teaspoon (1.5 grams) salt

1 cup plus 2 tablespoons (136 grams) all-purpose flour

1 teaspoon (4 grams) baking soda

1 tablespoon (15 grams) milk

FOR THE SPICE COATING

2 tablespoons (25 grams) granulated sugar

½ teaspoon (1 gram) cinnamon

¼ teaspoon ground cardamom

¼ teaspoon ground ginger

¼ teaspoon ground cloves

¼ teaspoon ground allspice

¼ teaspoon black pepper

TO MAKE THE COOKIES

1. Preheat the oven to 350°F. Line two sheet pans with parchment paper.

2. In a large bowl, combine the melted butter, brown sugar, and granulated sugar. Add the egg, vanilla, salt, flour, and baking soda, and mix with a spatula. Add the milk last. Chill the dough in the refrigerator for 20 minutes to make scooping easier.

TO MAKE THE SPICE COATING

3. In a small bowl, combine the sugar and all the spices. Mix with a fork to combine.

4. Use a soup spoon to scoop out roughly 2 tablespoons of dough. Form the dough into a ball, roll it in the sugar and spice coating, and then place it on one of the sheet pans. Repeat with the rest of the dough. Space the dough 4 inches apart, as these cookies spread.

5. Bake the cookies for 10 minutes. Transfer to a wire rack and cool for 30 minutes. Store in an airtight container.

Double Chocolate Chunk Brownies

MAKES 6 BROWNIES **BAKING VESSEL:** LOAF PAN

Prep Time: 10 minutes, plus 2 hours to cool / **Cook Time:** 30 minutes

The question is not whether you love brownies but rather if you prefer them with nuts or without. I prefer mine studded with more chocolate, but if you are on Team Nut, add ½ cup of your favorite chopped nut and fold it into the batter just before baking. This brownie recipe is fudgy, rich, and perfect for when that chocolate craving hits.

Nonstick baking spray

8 tablespoons (113 grams) unsalted butter

¾ cup (120 grams) semisweet chocolate chips

2 eggs

½ cup (100 grams) granulated sugar

½ teaspoon (3 grams) salt

½ cup (64 grams) all-purpose flour

½ cup (80 grams) chocolate chunks

1. Preheat the oven to 350°F. Lightly spray a loaf pan with nonstick baking spray, and then line it with parchment paper, allowing some parchment to go up 2 inches on the sides.

2. In a medium microwave-safe bowl, combine the butter and chocolate chips. Microwave in 30-second increments until they're fully melted, stirring after each increment. Once melted, stir in the eggs and sugar until smooth. Add the salt and flour, then stir until smooth.

3. Pour the batter into the prepared loaf pan and sprinkle the chocolate chunks over the top. Bake the brownies for 25 to 30 minutes, or until the center appears set and does not jiggle.

4. Let them cool in the pan for 1 to 2 hours until completely cool, then lift them out of the pan and onto a cutting board by holding the ends of the parchment paper. Cut into six brownies by cutting in half lengthwise and then into thirds widthwise. Store in an airtight container.

Peanut Butter Blondies

MAKES 6 BARS **BAKING VESSEL:** LOAF PAN

Prep Time: 10 minutes, plus 2 hours to cool / **Cook Time:** 25 minutes

When a butterscotch pudding meets a dessert bar, you get a blondie. Any dessert that starts with brown sugar and butter is always going to taste delicious, and this bar is only improved by America's favorite nut butter: peanut! Slightly salted, with a little crunch from fresh peanuts, this bar will have you going back for bite after bite. You may want a cold glass of milk with this one.

Nonstick baking spray

2 tablespoons (28 grams) unsalted butter, melted

6 tablespoons (85 grams) peanut butter

½ cup (100 grams) packed light brown sugar

1 teaspoon (6 grams) vanilla extract

1 egg

½ cup (64 grams) all-purpose flour

½ cup (75 grams) chopped unsalted peanuts

1. Preheat the oven to 350°F. Lightly spray a loaf pan with nonstick baking spray, and then line it with parchment paper, allowing some parchment to go up 2 inches on the sides.

2. In a medium bowl, combine the melted butter, peanut butter, brown sugar, and vanilla. Mix with a spatula. Add the egg and mix until combined. Add the flour and mix until combined; then, fold in the peanuts.

3. Pour the batter into the loaf pan and smooth it out evenly with a spatula. Bake the blondies for 20 to 25 minutes, or until the center appears set and does not jiggle.

4. Let them cool in the pan at room temperature for 1 to 2 hours until completely cool; then, lift them out of the pan onto a cutting board by holding the ends of the parchment paper. Cut into six bars by cutting in half lengthwise and then into thirds widthwise. Store in an airtight container.

VARIATION TIP: For gluten-free blondies, swap out the all-purpose flour for any cup-for-cup gluten-free flour. Look for gluten-free flour that has xanthan gum in the blend, as it helps with binding.

Carrot Cake Bars with Cream Cheese Swirl

MAKES 6 BARS **BAKING VESSEL:** LOAF PAN

Prep Time: 15 minutes, plus 1 hour to cool / **Cook Time:** 30 minutes

In my opinion, carrot cake and cream cheese go together like peanut butter and jelly. If you have a food processor, you can pulse the carrots in the machine faster than you can shred them by hand.

FOR THE CREAM CHEESE SWIRL

½ cup (60 grams) cream cheese, at room temperature

2 tablespoons (25 grams) granulated sugar

Pinch salt

FOR THE CARROT CAKE

Nonstick baking spray

4 tablespoons (56 grams) unsalted butter, melted

1 teaspoon (2 grams) cinnamon

½ cup (100 grams) granulated sugar

¼ teaspoon (1.5 grams) salt

1 egg

½ teaspoon (2 grams) baking soda

½ cup (64 grams) all-purpose flour

¾ cup shredded carrots (1 to 2 carrots)

TO MAKE THE CREAM CHEESE SWIRL

1. In a small bowl, combine the cream cheese, sugar, and salt. Stir with a spatula until the mixture is smooth. Set aside.

TO MAKE THE CARROT CAKE

2. Preheat the oven to 350°F. Lightly spray a loaf pan with nonstick baking spray, and then line it with parchment paper, allowing some parchment to go up 2 inches on the sides.

3. In a medium bowl, combine the melted butter, cinnamon, sugar, and salt. Whisk until smooth. Add the egg and whisk to combine. Use a spatula to stir in the baking soda and flour. Fold just until the batter is smooth. Fold in the carrots last. Pour the batter into the prepared loaf pan.

4. Drop spoonfuls of the cream cheese swirl into the carrot cake batter. Take a toothpick and swirl the cream cheese into the batter.

5. Bake the carrot cake for 30 minutes. Put the pan in the refrigerator and let it cool for 1 hour. Lift the cake out of the pan onto a cutting board by holding the ends of the parchment paper. Cut into six bars by cutting in half lengthwise and then into thirds widthwise. Store in an airtight container.

VARIATION TIP: Substitute an equal amount of shredded zucchini for the shredded carrots for a different twist.

Raspberry Oatmeal Almond Crumb Bars

MAKES 6 BARS **BAKING VESSEL:** LOAF PAN

Prep Time: 15 minutes, plus 2 hours to cool / **Cook Time:** 45 minutes

I like to think of these as breakfast bars. They have all the makings of a great breakfast—oats, nuts, fruit—and are perfect for on the go. This recipe is easy to make in a food processor, but if you don't have one, you can also mix it with a fork. Simply add all ingredients to a large bowl and work the mixture with the fork until it is evenly crumbly. This may take a little longer, but the end result is worth it.

FOR THE RASPBERRY FILLING

1 pint (6 ounces [170 g]) fresh raspberries

1 tablespoon (8 grams) cornstarch

2 tablespoons (25 grams) granulated sugar

1 tablespoon (15 grams) lemon juice

FOR THE OATMEAL ALMOND CRUMB

Nonstick baking spray

½ cup (78 grams) rolled oats

1 cup (120 grams) all-purpose flour

½ cup (75 grams) chopped almonds

1 tablespoon (12 grams) granulated sugar

2 tablespoons (28 grams) packed light brown sugar

¼ teaspoon (1 gram) baking powder

⅛ teaspoon salt

7 tablespoons (99 grams) unsalted butter, cold

1 egg yolk

TO MAKE THE RASPBERRY FILLING

1. In a medium bowl, combine the raspberries, cornstarch, sugar, and lemon juice. Toss with a spatula until the fruit is evenly coated, breaking up the raspberries a little. Set aside.

TO MAKE THE OATMEAL ALMOND CRUMB

2. Preheat the oven to 350°F. Lightly spray a loaf pan with nonstick baking spray, and then line it with parchment paper, allowing some parchment to go up 2 inches on the sides.

3. Combine the oats, flour, almonds, granulated sugar, brown sugar, baking powder, salt, butter, and egg yolk in a food processor. Process until the butter is fully incorporated and mixture appears crumbly. Or combine all the ingredients in a large bowl and mix with a fork until the mixture is evenly crumbly.

4. Pour half the crumb mixture into the loaf pan and press down firmly in an even layer. Pour all the raspberry filling over the base in an even layer. Sprinkle the remaining crumb mixture over the filling in an even layer. Press down slightly but not too hard.

5. Bake the bars for 45 minutes. Cool in pan for 1 to 2 hours at room temperature until they are completely cool. Use the parchment paper to lift out the bars from the pan and place on a cutting board. Cut into six bars by cutting in half lengthwise and then into thirds widthwise. Store in an airtight container.

VARIATION TIP: The raspberries can easily be switched out for strawberries, blueberries, blackberries, or even chopped rhubarb. You can also replace the almonds with your favorite nut. The possible combinations are endless!

Millionaire Shortbread Bars with Caramel and Chocolate Ganache

MAKES 6 BARS **BAKING VESSEL:** LOAF PAN

Prep Time: 25 minutes, plus 2 hours to chill / **Cook Time:** 20 minutes

This chocolate-caramel-shortbread bar is truly decadent and rich, and that is how it got the name "millionaire." With one bite you'll get three layers of heaven. To kick it up a notch, you can add a layer of chopped nuts after the caramel layer and before the chocolate ganache. If you do, however, you'll likely want to call it billionaire shortbread.

FOR THE SHORTBREAD

Nonstick baking spray

6 tablespoons (85 grams) unsalted butter, at room temperature

2 tablespoons (28 grams) packed light brown sugar

2 tablespoons (25 grams) granulated sugar

1 egg yolk

¾ cup (96 grams) all-purpose flour

¼ teaspoon (1.5 grams) salt

FOR THE CARAMEL

1 cup (306 grams) sweetened condensed milk

2 tablespoons (41 grams) corn syrup

4 tablespoons (56 grams) unsalted butter

⅓ cup (65 grams) packed light brown sugar

¼ teaspoon (1.5 grams) salt

FOR THE CHOCOLATE GANACHE

½ cup (85 grams) semisweet chocolate chips

⅓ cup (85 grams) heavy cream

TO MAKE THE SHORTBREAD

1. Preheat the oven to 350°F. Lightly spray a loaf pan with nonstick baking spray, and then line it with parchment paper, allowing some parchment to go up 2 inches on the sides.

2. In a stand mixer fitted with the paddle attachment or a handheld electric mixer and a large bowl, combine the butter, brown sugar, and granulated sugar. Add the egg yolk, flour, and salt, and mix until smooth.

3. Press the shortbread evenly into the loaf pan. Bake for 15 to 18 minutes, or until the edges are light golden brown. Cool in the pan at room temperature for 20 minutes while you make the caramel.

TO MAKE THE CARAMEL

4. In a large skillet over medium heat, combine the condensed milk, corn syrup, butter, brown sugar, and salt. When the butter is melted, stir and cook for 6 to 8 minutes, or until the caramel has thickened. Pour the caramel over the shortbread in the pan.

5. Put the pan in the refrigerator to chill for 1 hour.

TO MAKE THE CHOCOLATE GANACHE

6. In a microwave-safe bowl, combine the chocolate chips and heavy cream, and microwave in 30-second increments, stirring after each increment, until the mixture is fully melted and smooth. Pour the ganache evenly over the chilled caramel layer, and return the pan to the refrigerator for 1 more hour.

7. Use the parchment paper to lift the shortbread out of the pan onto a cutting board. Cut into six bars by cutting in half lengthwise and then into thirds widthwise. Store in an airtight container in the refrigerator.

BAKING TIP: Making caramel is easy, but it can burn if left unattended. Make sure you stir frequently and do not step away in the middle of the process.

STICKY TOFFEE PUDDING CAKE WITH BOURBON TOFFEE SAUCE

CHAPTER 5
cakes *and* shortcakes

Almond Olive Oil Cake with Honey-Thyme Glaze

Chocolate Cake with Raspberry Jam Filling

Buttermilk Roulade Cake with Mascarpone Berry Filling

Sticky Toffee Pudding Cake with Bourbon Toffee Sauce

S'mores Layer Cake

Chocolate Lava Cakes

Strawberry Shortcakes with Lemon Whipped Cream

Whole-Wheat Oat Shortcakes with Apples and Whipped Cream

Almond Olive Oil Cake with Honey-Thyme Glaze

MAKES 6 SLICES **BAKING VESSEL:** LOAF PAN

Prep Time: 10 minutes, plus 2 hours to cool / **Cook Time:** 25 minutes

Olive oil in cake? Why, yes! I was first introduced to olive oil cake early in my career as a pastry chef. I had often used vegetable oil in my cakes but had never even considered olive oil. I came to find out the practice has been around for years! Olive oil cake has a long history in the Mediterranean, probably because the best olive oil comes from that area. The texture is delicate, and the flavor is lightly fruity, just like olive oil. It has quickly become a favorite.

FOR THE CAKE

Nonstick baking spray

¼ cup (32 grams) olive oil

⅓ cup (67 grams) granulated sugar

1 egg

1 egg yolk

¼ cup (85 grams) milk

1 teaspoon (2 grams) lemon zest

½ teaspoon (3 grams) vanilla extract

¼ teaspoon (1 gram) almond extract (optional)

½ cup (60 grams) all-purpose flour

⅓ cup (32 grams) almond flour

¾ teaspoon (3 grams) baking powder

¼ teaspoon (1.5 grams) salt

FOR THE GLAZE

1 cup (115 grams) powdered sugar, sifted

1 tablespoon (21 grams) honey

2 tablespoons (30 grams) milk

1 teaspoon (1 gram) chopped fresh thyme

TO MAKE THE CAKE

1. Preheat the oven to 350°F. Lightly spray a loaf pan with nonstick baking spray, and then line it with parchment paper, allowing some parchment to go up 2 inches on the sides.

2. To make the cake, in a large bowl, whisk together the olive oil and sugar. Add the egg, yolk, milk, zest, vanilla extract, and almond extract (if using), and whisk until smooth. Then add the all-purpose flour, almond flour, baking powder, and salt. Fold with a spatula until well mixed.

3. Pour the batter into the loaf pan. Bake for 25 minutes, or until a toothpick inserted in the center comes out clean. Let the cake cool in the pan for 20 minutes. Lift the cake out of the loaf pan by picking up the sides of the parchment paper. Carefully remove the paper and cool completely on a wire rack, about 30 minutes.

TO MAKE THE GLAZE

4. Combine the powdered sugar, honey, milk, and thyme in a medium bowl. Whisk until smooth. Place a piece of parchment paper under the wire rack with the cake. Pour the glaze over the entire surface of the cooled cake, and cool at room temperature for 1 hour.

5. To serve, cut the cake in half lengthwise and in thirds widthwise, yielding six slices.

INGREDIENT TIP: Olive oil is expensive. Don't waste your extra-virgin olive oil in baking; use regular olive oil.

Chocolate Cake with Raspberry Jam Filling

MAKES 6 SLICES **BAKING VESSEL:** 8-INCH-SQUARE BAKING PAN

Prep Time: 20 minutes, plus 2 hours to chill and 1 hour to set / **Cook Time:** 30 minutes

This cake is not only easy to make—it's also dairy-free and vegan! We all have friends in our lives who have food sensitivities, and those friends deserve a slice of chocolate cake, too. There are no special dairy-free or vegan ingredients required—just the same standard baking staples you'll likely already have in your pantry.

FOR THE CAKE

Nonstick baking spray

⅓ cup (80 grams) canola oil

1 teaspoon (6 grams) vanilla extract

1 cup (200 grams) granulated sugar

½ teaspoon (3 grams) salt

1½ cups (180 grams) all-purpose flour

¼ cup (25 grams) unsweetened cocoa powder

1 teaspoon (6 grams) baking soda

1 cup (236 grams) water

1 tablespoon (14 grams) white vinegar

¼ cup (56 grams) raspberry jam

1 pint (6 ounces [170 grams]) fresh raspberries

FOR THE ICING

1½ cups (170 grams) powdered sugar, sifted

2 tablespoons (15 grams) unsweetened cocoa powder

Pinch salt

3 tablespoons (45 grams) water

1 tablespoon (20 grams) corn syrup

TO MAKE THE CAKE

1. Preheat the oven to 350°F. Lightly spray an 8-inch-square baking pan with nonstick baking spray, and then line it with parchment paper, allowing some parchment to go up 2 inches on the sides.

2. In a large bowl, whisk together the oil, vanilla, sugar, and salt. Fold in the flour, cocoa powder, and baking soda. Add the water and vinegar last and stir with a spatula until the batter is very smooth.

3. Pour the batter into the baking pan and bake for 30 minutes, or until a toothpick inserted in the center comes out clean. Keep the cake in the pan and put it in the freezer until it's very cold, 1 to 2 hours.

4. Line a sheet pan with parchment paper and place a wire rack on it. To assemble the cake, run a knife around the edges and lift the cake from the pan. Place it on a cutting board. Cut it in half down the middle, yielding two 4-by-8-inch pieces.

5. Place one piece of cake on the wire rack. Spread the raspberry jam over the top of the cake, smoothing it out with a spoon to make an even layer of jam. Top with the fresh raspberries. Put the second piece of cake on top of the raspberry layer.

TO MAKE THE ICING

6. Whisk the powdered sugar, cocoa powder, salt, water, and corn syrup in a medium bowl until very smooth.

7. Slowly pour the icing evenly over the cake, covering all the edges. Let the icing dry at room temperature for 1 hour.

8. Transfer the cake to a serving tray or refrigerate up to 3 days.

VARIATION TIP: If you're not a fan of raspberries, a great alternative is peanut butter. Layer the cake with ¼ cup (60 grams) of smooth peanut butter and ¼ cup (40 grams) of chopped peanuts for an extra crunch.

Buttermilk Roulade Cake with Mascarpone Berry Filling

MAKES *6 SLICES* **BAKING VESSEL:** *9-BY-13-INCH BAKING PAN*

Prep Time: 20 minutes, plus 1 hour to cool and 4 hours to chill /
Cook Time: 10 minutes

Roulade cakes, also known as Swiss rolls, are always impressive. They can be a little daunting, but a good tip is to make sure you have a tea towel dusted with powdered sugar ready to go when your cake comes out of the oven. It's important to roll the cake up in the towel while it's warm, so you don't tear it later.

FOR THE CAKE

Nonstick baking spray

2 egg whites

½ cup (100 grams) granulated sugar, divided

2 egg yolks

3 tablespoons (45 grams) buttermilk

½ cup (60 grams) all-purpose flour

¾ cup (50 grams) powdered sugar, divided

½ teaspoon (2 grams) baking powder

⅛ teaspoon salt

FOR THE FILLING

½ cup (91 grams) mascarpone cheese

½ cup (113 grams) heavy cream

2 tablespoons (25 grams) granulated sugar

½ teaspoon (3 grams) vanilla extract

½ cup (95 grams) fresh berries

TO MAKE THE CAKE

1. Preheat the oven to 375°F. Lightly spray a 9-by-13-inch baking pan with nonstick baking spray. Line it with parchment paper, allowing the paper to go up 2 inches on the sides.

2. In a stand mixer fitted with the whisk attachment or using a handheld electric mixer and a medium bowl, whisk the egg whites and ¼ cup (50 grams) of granulated sugar into stiff peaks. Transfer to a large bowl and set aside.

3. Returning the bowl to the stand mixer or using your handheld mixer again, add the egg yolks and remaining ¼ cup (50 grams) of granulated sugar and whip on high speed until the yolks are thick and lighter in color. Add the buttermilk and mix until it's fully incorporated. Remove the bowl from the stand and fold in the flour, ¼ cup (25 grams) of powdered sugar, the baking powder, and the salt. Fold the egg white mixture into the batter last.

4. Pour the batter into the baking pan and spread it out evenly with a spatula. Bake for 10 minutes.

5. While the cake is baking, set up a tea towel on a work surface. Dust it thoroughly with ¼ cup (50 grams) of powdered sugar so the cake doesn't stick. When the cake comes out of the oven, immediately lift it out of the baking pan using the parchment paper. Flip it over onto the tea towel. Peel back the paper and discard it. Immediately roll the cake up in the towel. Let it cool at room temperature for 1 hour, or until completely cooled.

TO MAKE THE FILLING AND FINISH THE CAKE

6. In the bowl of a stand mixer fitted with the whisk attachment or in a large bowl with a handheld electric mixer, combine the mascarpone, cream, sugar, and vanilla. Whip on medium speed until stiff peaks form. Add the fresh berries and mix until they have broken up a little and are evenly spread out in the filling.

7. To assemble the cake, carefully unroll it from the tea towel. Place the filling in the center of the cake and smooth it out evenly with a spatula. Reroll the cake and place it on a serving tray. Chill in the refrigerator for 4 or more hours.

8. To serve, dust the remaining ¼ cup (50 grams) of powdered sugar over the entire top of the cake. Cut into six slices.

Sticky Toffee Pudding Cake with Bourbon Toffee Sauce

MAKES 6 SLICES **BAKING VESSEL:** 8-INCH-SQUARE BAKING PAN

Prep Time: 20 minutes, plus 2 hours to cool / **Cook Time:** 25 minutes

There's nothing better or more decadent than sticky toffee pudding—except maybe when it's made with bourbon! This cake is made by softening dates in water and then blending them. If you don't have a blender, you can just chop the dates up into little pieces and then add them and the water directly to the batter.

FOR THE CAKE

Nonstick baking spray

1 cup (120 grams) pitted and chopped dates

1 cup (236 grams) water

¼ cup (56 grams) unsalted butter, melted

¼ cup (50 grams) granulated sugar

¼ cup (50 grams) packed light brown sugar

1 egg

1 tablespoon (20 grams) molasses

½ teaspoon (3 grams) salt

¾ teaspoon (3 grams) baking soda

1 cup (120 grams) all-purpose flour

FOR THE SAUCE

¼ cup (56 grams) unsalted butter

¼ cup (56 grams) cream

½ cup (100 grams) packed light brown sugar

1 tablespoon (20 grams) molasses

¼ teaspoon (1.5 grams) salt

½ teaspoon (3 grams) vanilla extract

¼ cup (56 grams) bourbon whiskey

TO MAKE THE CAKE

1. Preheat the oven to 350°F. Line the bottom of an 8-inch-square baking pan with parchment paper. Spray the entire pan with nonstick baking spray.

2. In a small saucepan over medium heat, combine the dates and water, and heat to a boil. Transfer the mixture to a blender, and blend until smooth. Pour the mixture into a large bowl. Add the melted butter, granulated sugar, and brown sugar, and whisk until smooth. Add the egg and molasses, and whisk. Add the salt, baking soda, and flour last, and fold until smooth.

3. Pour the batter into the baking pan and spread it out evenly with a spatula. Bake for 20 to 25 minutes, or until a toothpick inserted in the center comes out clean. Prepare the bourbon toffee sauce while the cake is baking.

TO MAKE THE SAUCE

4. In a small saucepan over medium heat, combine the butter, cream, brown sugar, molasses, salt, and vanilla. Heat until everything is melted, and then boil for 2 to 3 minutes, or until the sauce appears to thicken a little. Remove from the heat and stir in the bourbon.

5. When the cake comes out of the oven, immediately pour the bourbon toffee sauce evenly over the top. Let the cake soak and cool down for 2 hours before serving.

6. Cut the cake down the middle in half, and then rotate the pan and cut into thirds, yielding six slices.

INGREDIENT TIP: Dates can come pitted or not pitted, so make sure yours are pitted before adding them to this recipe. If you happen to have dates with pits, just slice into them and remove the pits before boiling them.

S'mores Layer Cake

MAKES 6 SLICES **BAKING VESSEL:** 9-BY-13-INCH BAKING PAN

Prep Time: 25 minutes, plus 1 hour to chill / **Cook Time:** 25 minutes

When I think of s'mores, I'm always transported back to my Girl Scout days when we would go camping and make s'mores by the fire. Those were the good old days!

FOR THE CAKE

Nonstick baking spray

¼ cup graham cracker crumbs

½ cup plus 2 tablespoons (76 grams) all-purpose flour

½ teaspoon (2 grams) baking powder

¼ teaspoon (1 gram) baking soda

¼ teaspoon (1.5 grams) salt

½ teaspoon (1 gram) cinnamon

⅛ teaspoon ground allspice

¼ cup (56 grams) buttermilk

¼ cup (56 grams) sour cream

½ cup (113 grams) unsalted butter, at room temperature

¼ cup (50 grams) packed light brown sugar

¼ cup (50 grams) granulated sugar

2 eggs

FOR THE FILLINGS

⅓ cup (40 grams) cream

½ cup (85 grams) semisweet chocolate chips

¼ cup (56 grams) unsalted butter, at room temperature

½ cup (50 grams) powdered sugar

½ cup (70 grams) marshmallow fluff

1 teaspoon (6 grams) vanilla extract

½ cup (30 grams) mini marshmallows

TO MAKE THE CAKE

1. Preheat the oven to 350°F. Lightly spray a 9-by-13-inch baking pan with nonstick baking spray, and then line the bottom with parchment paper.

2. In a medium bowl, combine the graham cracker crumbs, flour, baking powder, baking soda, salt, cinnamon, and allspice. In a small bowl, combine the buttermilk and sour cream. Set both bowls aside.

3. In a stand mixer fitted with the paddle attachment or using a large bowl and handheld mixer, cream the butter, brown sugar, and granulated sugar until smooth. Add the eggs and mix well. Then alternate adding dry and wet ingredients from the other bowls into the batter. Scrape down the sides as needed. Mix until smooth.

4. Pour the batter into the baking pan and use a spatula to even out the cake. Bake for 20 minutes, or until a toothpick inserted in the center comes out clean.

5. When cake comes out of the oven, immediately put it in the freezer. Freeze for 1 hour until it's firm enough to cut and layer. Meanwhile, make the fillings.

TO MAKE THE FILLINGS

6. Make the chocolate ganache layer first. In a microwave-safe bowl, heat the cream and chocolate chips in the microwave for 30 seconds. Stir, and then heat for another 30 seconds. Stir until the mixture is smooth. Chill the ganache in the refrigerator, uncovered, for 30 minutes.

7. To make the marshmallow frosting, combine the butter and powdered sugar in a stand mixer fitted with the paddle attachment, or use a handheld mixer and a medium bowl. Mix on low to combine, and then add the marshmallow fluff and vanilla. Scrape down the sides as needed and mix until smooth. Transfer the marshmallow frosting to a piping bag or a zip-top bag with the bottom corner snipped off, and set aside until needed.

TO ASSEMBLE THE CAKE

8. Remove the cake from the freezer and invert it onto a cutting board. Cut all the edges off. Remove the parchment and cut the cake in half lengthwise and then widthwise so you have four pieces.

9. Place one piece on a serving tray. Spoon 1 tablespoon of chocolate ganache on top, and use the spoon to evenly spread the ganache over this layer. Next, pipe a layer of marshmallow frosting over the ganache. Top the frosting with a second layer of cake. Repeat the same order of fillings, leaving the last piece of cake clean on the top. You should use up all the marshmallow frosting but still have about 2 tablespoons of ganache left over.

10. Microwave the remaining ganache for 20 seconds, until it's loose enough to drizzle. Transfer the ganache to a piping bag or a zip-top bag with the bottom corner snipped off, and drizzle it over the entire top layer of the cake. Garnish with the mini marshmallows. If you have a kitchen blowtorch, use it to toast the mini marshmallows. (They're fine untoasted if you don't have a blowtorch.)

11. Chill the cake until you're ready to serve. To serve, slice 1-inch-square pieces of cake.

VARIATION TIP: Give this cake a gingerbread twist when the winter months roll around. Add 1 tablespoon (5 grams) of ground ginger to the dry ingredients and 1 tablespoon (20 grams) of molasses to the wet ingredients in step 2 when making the cake. Prepare the rest as directed.

Chocolate Lava Cakes

MAKES 6 CAKES **BAKING VESSEL:** MUFFIN TIN

Prep Time: 15 minutes / **Cook Time:** 15 minutes

Chocolate lava cakes are rich, gooey, and delicious. This was one of the first desserts I ever learned how to make, and it's become a classic for me. The key is to bake the cake at a high temperature so the outside is firm and the inside remains a creamy chocolate lava.

Nonstick baking spray

Unsweetened cocoa powder, for dusting

½ cup (56 grams) unsalted butter

1 cup (170 grams) semisweet chocolate chips

½ cup (50 grams) powdered sugar, sifted

⅛ teaspoon salt

2 eggs

2 egg yolks

¼ cup (34 grams) all-purpose flour

1. Preheat the oven to 425°F. Spray a muffin tin with nonstick baking spray. Dust the muffin cups with cocoa powder.

2. Put the butter and chocolate chips in a large microwave-safe bowl. Microwave in 30-second increments, stirring after each increment, until the mixture is fully melted and smooth. Whisk in the powdered sugar, salt, eggs, and yolks until smooth. Fold in the flour last.

3. Scoop the batter into the muffin cups, filling them all the way to the top. Bake for 8 to 9 minutes, or until the cake does not appear liquid.

4. Remove from the oven and cool the cakes in the pan at room temperature for 5 minutes. Invert the muffin tin onto a cutting board or sheet pan to remove the cakes. Use a spatula to transfer the cakes to serving plates. Serve immediately.

BAKING TIP: This cake batter can be made up to a week ahead of time. When you're ready to serve, simply grease and dust the muffin tin with cocoa powder and scoop the batter inside. Bake and serve as directed.

Strawberry Shortcakes with Lemon Whipped Cream

MAKES 6 SHORTCAKES **BAKING VESSEL:** SHEET PAN

Prep Time: 25 minutes / **Cook Time:** 15 minutes

Summer calls for lighter desserts, and nothing is quite as classic as strawberry shortcake. A shortcake is a small cake made of biscuit dough, and you will see the same laminating (folding and rolling) technique here that you used for the biscuits in chapter 2. Blackberries, blueberries, and raspberries are all great variations to use for this recipe. Swap out the same quantity of berries and prepare as directed.

FOR THE SHORTCAKES

2 cups (240 grams) all-purpose flour, plus more for rolling

1 tablespoon (14 grams) baking powder

2 tablespoons (25 grams) granulated sugar

½ teaspoon (3 grams) salt

5 tablespoons (70 grams) unsalted butter, cold, cubed

¾ cup (182 grams) buttermilk

FOR THE STRAWBERRY COMPOTE

2 cups (400 grams) hulled and quartered fresh strawberries

1 tablespoon (14 grams) lemon juice

½ teaspoon (3 grams) vanilla extract

2 tablespoons (25 grams) granulated sugar

FOR THE LEMON WHIPPED CREAM

¾ cup (180 grams) heavy cream

3 tablespoons (21 grams) powdered sugar

1 tablespoon (6 grams) lemon zest

TO MAKE THE SHORTCAKES

1. Preheat the oven to 425°F. Line a sheet pan with parchment paper.

2. In the bowl of a stand mixer fitted with the paddle attachment or using a large bowl and a handheld mixer, combine the flour, baking powder, sugar, and salt. Mix to combine. Add the cubed butter. Mix on low for 1 minute. Continue to mix on low and drizzle in the buttermilk. The dough should form together with some visible chunks of butter. Remove the dough from the mixer and place on a floured work surface.

3. Dust a rolling pin with flour and roll out the dough into a 12-by-16-inch rectangle. Fold one-third of the dough from the left side into the center. Then fold one-third from the right side over the other fold, creating a trifold. Roll out the dough again into a 12-by-16-inch rectangle and repeat the folds. Then do it one more time, for a total of three times. After the third set of folds, you should have a 6-by-8-inch rectangle. Cut it into six pieces by cutting it in half lengthwise and then cutting each half across in thirds.

4. Place the shortcakes evenly on the lined sheet pan, spaced about 2 inches apart. Freeze the dough for 5 minutes.

5. Bake the shortcakes for 15 minutes, or until they're puffed up and evenly browned. Let the shortcakes cool at room temperature while you're making the strawberry compote and lemon whipped cream.

TO MAKE THE STRAWBERRY COMPOTE

6. Combine the strawberries, lemon juice, vanilla, and sugar in a medium bowl. Toss with a spatula until the fruit is evenly coated, and let it sit at room temperature while preparing the whipped cream.

TO MAKE THE LEMON WHIPPED CREAM AND FINISH THE SHORTCAKES

7. In a stand mixer fitted with the whisk attachment or using a handheld mixer with a medium bowl, whip the cream, powdered sugar, and lemon zest until medium peaks form.

8. To assemble, cut each shortcake in half across. On the bottom half, spoon some strawberry compote. Top with a dollop of whipped cream and then the top half of the shortcake. Repeat for the remaining shortcakes. Serve immediately.

Whole-Wheat Oat Shortcakes with Apples and Whipped Cream

MAKES 6 SHORTCAKES   **BAKING VESSEL:** SHEET PAN

Prep Time: 25 minutes / **Cook Time:** 25 minutes

An apple is one of the most versatile fruits out there. On its own, it can be a healthy snack dipped in peanut butter, sprinkled with cinnamon, or eaten just by itself. An apple can be baked in a pie or cooked into apple sauce, and here it's the perfect filling for hearty whole-wheat shortcakes. Not all apples are created equal—for baking, anyway. Each variety has its own texture and flavor. This recipe calls for green apples, such as Granny Smith, but some other great baking apples include Jonagold, Honeycrisp, Pink Lady, and Braeburn.

FOR THE SHORTCAKES

1 cup (120 grams) all-purpose flour, plus more for rolling

¾ cup (90 grams) whole-wheat flour

½ cup (45 grams) rolled oats

1 tablespoon (14 grams) baking powder

2 tablespoons (25 grams) granulated sugar

½ teaspoon (3 grams) salt

5 tablespoons (70 grams) unsalted butter, cold, cubed

¾ cup (184 grams) milk

FOR THE TOFFEE APPLE FILLING

2 green apples (236 grams), peeled, cored, and diced

1 tablespoon (14 grams) lemon juice

¼ cup (56 grams) unsalted butter

¼ cup (50 grams) packed light brown sugar

1 teaspoon (6 grams) vanilla extract

⅛ teaspoon salt

1 tablespoon (14 grams) cream

FOR THE WHIPPED CREAM

¾ cup (180 grams) heavy cream

3 tablespoons (21 grams) powdered sugar, sifted

1 teaspoon (6 grams) vanilla extract

TO MAKE THE SHORTCAKES

1. Preheat the oven to 425°F. Line a sheet pan with parchment paper.

2. In the bowl of a stand mixer fitted with the paddle attachment or using a handheld mixer and a large bowl, combine the all-purpose flour, whole-wheat flour, oats, baking powder, sugar, and salt. Mix to combine. Add the cubed butter. Mix on low for 1 minute. Continue to mix on low and drizzle in the milk. The dough should form together with some visible chunks of butter. Remove the dough from the mixer and place on a floured work surface.

3. Dust a rolling pin with flour and roll out the dough into a 12-by-16-inch rectangle. Fold one-third of the dough from the left side into the center. Then fold one-third from the right side over the other fold, creating a trifold. Roll out the dough again into a 12-by-16-inch rectangle and repeat the folds. Then do it one more time, for a total of three times. After the third set of folds, you should have a 6-by-8-inch rectangle. Cut it into six pieces by cutting it in half lengthwise and then cutting each half across in thirds.

4. Place the shortcakes evenly on the lined sheet pan, spaced about 2 inches apart. Chill the dough in the refrigerator for 10 minutes.

5. Bake the shortcakes for 15 minutes, or until they're puffed up and evenly browned. Let the shortcakes cool at room temperature while you're making the toffee apple filling and vanilla whipped cream.

TO MAKE THE TOFFEE APPLE FILLING

6. Put the apples in a large bowl and sprinkle with the lemon juice. Toss to coat.

7. In a large skillet, heat the butter until it's melted. Add the apples, brown sugar, vanilla, and salt. Cook for 3 to 4 minutes, until the apples are caramelized. Stir in the cream and cook for another 3 minutes. The sauce should be slightly thickened. Transfer the mixture to a medium bowl and set aside until needed.

TO MAKE THE WHIPPED CREAM AND FINISH THE SHORTCAKES

8. In a stand mixer fitted with the whisk attachment or using a handheld mixer and a medium bowl, whip the cream, powdered sugar, and vanilla until medium peaks form.

9. To assemble, cut each shortcake in half across. On the bottom half, spoon some toffee apple filling. Top with a dollop of whipped cream and then the top half of the shortcake. Repeat for the remaining shortcakes. Serve immediately.

VARIATION TIP: Peach shortcake is a favorite of mine during the summer months. To make this variation, substitute the same amount of peaches as apples, and make the recipe as directed.

HAZELNUT, CHOCOLATE, AND CARAMEL TART

CHAPTER 6
pies, tarts, *and* quiche

Brown Sugar Butter Pie Crust

Everything but the Bagel Pie Crust

Cherry Pistachio Streusel Pie

Mini Pumpkin Pies

Greek Yogurt Berry Tart

Hazelnut, Chocolate, and Caramel Tart

Strawberry Rhubarb Mini Galette

Mini Pizza Quiche with Pepperoni, Mozzarella, and Olives

Mini Bacon and Cheese Quiche

Mushroom, Spinach, and Feta Quiche

Brown Sugar Butter Pie Crust

MAKES 1 SMALL SWEET CRUST

Prep Time: 5 minutes, plus 30 minutes to chill

Pie crust is my specialty. I've written two pie cookbooks and have made pie dough every which way. To make a flaky crust, it's imperative to use ice-cold butter and water while preparing the dough. Cut the butter into small cubes beforehand and put them in the freezer until you're ready to make the crust. Drop a few ice cubes into some water and let them chill the water before you use it.

¾ cup (96 grams) all-purpose flour

1½ tablespoons (18 grams) packed light brown sugar

¼ teaspoon (1.5 grams) salt

5 tablespoons (70 grams) unsalted butter, cold, cubed

2 tablespoons (28 grams) ice water

1. In a standard-size food processor, combine the flour, brown sugar, and salt. Add the cold butter and process for 20 seconds. While mixing, pour in 1 tablespoon of ice water, and then process for 20 seconds longer. Pour in the remaining tablespoon of ice water and process until the dough resembles wet crumbles.

2. Turn the dough out onto a clean work surface. Use your hands to form it into a disk, wrap with plastic wrap, and chill in the refrigerator for a minimum of 30 minutes before using.

BAKING TIP: The easiest way to make pie dough is in a food processor, but if you don't have one, you can certainly do it by hand. Combine all the ingredients except the water in a medium bowl. Cut in the butter with a pastry cutter or fork until the mixture appears crumbly. Drizzle in the ice water, 1 tablespoon at a time, while still working the dough with a fork. Once the dough starts to come together, follow the directions in step 2.

Everything but the Bagel Pie Crust

MAKES 1 SMALL SAVORY CRUST

Prep Time: 5 minutes, plus 30 minutes to chill

What can't you put everything bagel seasoning on? It's perfect on eggs, chicken, potatoes—you name it. I love using this seasoning in pie crust. It enhances the filling and smells so savory when it's being baked. To make your own everything bagel seasoning, mix together equal amounts of white sesame seeds, black sesame seeds, poppy seeds, dried onion flakes, dried minced garlic, and coarse sea salt or kosher salt. (For hand-mixing instructions, see Brown Sugar Butter Pie Crust.)

¾ cup (96 grams) all-purpose flour

1 teaspoon (4 grams) granulated sugar

1 tablespoon (12 grams) everything bagel seasoning

¼ teaspoon (1.5 grams) salt

5 tablespoons (70 grams) unsalted butter, cold, cubed

2 tablespoons (28 grams) ice water

1. In a standard-size food processor, combine the flour, sugar, seasoning, and salt. Add the cold butter and process for 20 seconds. While processing, pour in 1 tablespoon of ice water, and then process for 20 seconds longer. Pour in the remaining tablespoon of ice water and process until the dough resembles wet crumbles.

2. Turn the dough out onto a clean work surface. Use your hands to form it into a disk, wrap with plastic wrap, and chill in the refrigerator for a minimum of 30 minutes before using.

VARIATION TIP: Another way to make a great savory pie crust is to mix dry herbs into your dough. Simply swap out the everything bagel seasoning for dried herbs and make as directed.

Cherry Pistachio Streusel Pie

MAKES 6 SLICES **BAKING VESSEL:** 8-INCH-SQUARE BAKING PAN

Prep Time: 20 minutes, plus 2 hours to cool / **Cook Time:** 1 hour 10 minutes

Perfectly tart and sweet, cherry pie is one of my favorites. The sour-sweet cherry with salty, crunchy pistachio is a flavor duo that will keep you going back bite after bite.

FOR THE STREUSEL

⅓ cup (41 grams) chopped salted pistachios

¼ cup (22 grams) rolled oats

¼ cup (50 grams) packed light brown sugar

¼ cup (34 grams) all-purpose flour

4 tablespoons (56 grams) unsalted butter, melted

FOR THE PIE

Nonstick baking spray

All-purpose flour, for rolling

1 Brown Sugar Butter Pie Crust

3 cups (1¼ pounds) fresh cherries, pitted

2 tablespoons (15 grams) cornstarch

¼ cup (50 grams) granulated sugar

1 teaspoon (2 grams) lemon zest

2 tablespoons (28 grams) lemon juice

TO MAKE THE STREUSEL

1. Combine the pistachios, oats, brown sugar, flour, and butter in a medium bowl and mix until fully combined. Freeze until you're ready to make the pie.

TO MAKE THE PIE

2. Preheat the oven to 350°F. Lightly spray an 8-inch-square baking pan with nonstick baking spray.

3. Sprinkle some flour onto a clean work surface and roll out the dough to a 10-inch square. Flour the rolling pin and work surface as needed. Roll the dough onto the rolling pin and then out onto the baking pan. Press the dough into the corners and sides. Freeze the crust for 10 minutes.

4. In a medium bowl, combine the cherries, cornstarch, sugar, lemon zest, and lemon juice. Toss with a spatula until the fruit is evenly coated. Pour the filling into the crust and bake for 40 minutes. Sprinkle the streusel over the top, leaving some cherry filling showing, and bake for another 30 minutes.

5. Cool the pie at room temperature for 2 hours. Cut in half, and then turn the baking pan 45 degrees and cut each half into thirds for six slices.

INGREDIENT TIP: It's best to use fresh cherries whenever possible, but frozen cherries will work just fine. There's no need to adjust the time or temperature; just bake as directed.

Mini Pumpkin Pies

MAKES 6 MINI PIES BAKING VESSEL: MUFFIN TIN

Prep Time: 15 minutes, plus 20 minutes to cool / **Cook Time:** 30 minutes

Cooler temperatures usually mean it is pumpkin season. I'll admit it, I am one of those people who has to try every pumpkin spice treat, no matter what it is. There's no shame in my pumpkin game. Whenever you get that pumpkin craving, whether it be in November or in May, try these mini pies.

Nonstick baking spray

All-purpose flour, for rolling

1 Brown Sugar Butter Pie Crust

½ cup (60 grams) pumpkin puree

¼ cup (50 grams) granulated sugar

⅛ teaspoon salt

¼ teaspoon cinnamon

¼ teaspoon ground ginger

⅛ teaspoon ground cardamom

½ cup (113 grams) heavy cream

2 egg yolks

1 teaspoon (2.5 grams) cornstarch

½ teaspoon (3 grams) vanilla extract

1. Preheat the oven to 375°F. Lightly spray six cups of a muffin tin with nonstick baking spray.

2. Sprinkle some flour onto a clean work surface and roll out the dough to a 10-inch square. Flour the rolling pin and work surface as needed. Use a 4-inch-round cookie cutter to punch out four circles. Gather up the remaining dough and reroll it. Punch out two more circles. Fit each circle into a muffin tin cup. Freeze the mini crusts for 10 minutes.

3. In a medium bowl, whisk together the pumpkin, sugar, salt, cinnamon, ginger, cardamom, cream, egg yolks, cornstarch, and vanilla until fully blended. Pour the filling evenly into the pie crusts, filling them nearly all the way to the top.

4. Bake the pies for 30 minutes. Cool at room temperature for 20 minutes and serve.

BAKING TIP: To give these pies some extra flair, use the scrap dough you have left over to make cookie cutter leaves to top the pies. Simply roll out the scrap, punch out leaves, put them on a baking sheet lined with parchment paper, and bake at 350°F for 8 to 10 minutes. Top the mini pies with the leaves before serving.

Greek Yogurt Berry Tart

MAKES *6 SLICES* **BAKING VESSEL:** *8-INCH-SQUARE BAKING PAN*

Prep Time: 40 minutes, plus 2 hours to chill / **Cook Time:** 35 minutes

The delicate flavor of Greek yogurt pairs wonderfully with fresh berries in this no-bake filling. To enhance this dish even more, try using fresh vanilla beans. Simply swap out the vanilla extract for half of a vanilla bean pod, seeds scraped out, and prepare as directed.

Nonstick baking spray

All-purpose flour, for rolling

1 Brown Sugar Butter Pie Crust

3 tablespoons (42 grams) cold water

1 teaspoon (3 grams) unflavored powdered gelatin

1 cup (245 grams) plain Greek yogurt

½ cup (113 grams) cream

¼ cup (50 grams) granulated sugar

1 teaspoon (2 grams) lemon zest

½ teaspoon (3 grams) vanilla extract

¼ cup (48 grams) fresh raspberries

¼ cup (48 grams) fresh blackberries

¼ cup (48 grams) fresh blueberries

¼ cup (48 grams) fresh strawberries

1. Preheat the oven to 375°F. Lightly spray an 8-inch-square baking pan with nonstick baking spray.

2. Sprinkle some flour onto a clean work surface and roll out the dough to a 10-inch square. Flour the rolling pin and work surface as needed. Roll the dough onto the rolling pin and then out onto the baking pan. Press the dough into the corners and sides. Freeze the crust for 10 minutes while you make the filling.

3. Place a piece of parchment paper inside the crust. Add pie weights and bake the crust for 20 minutes. Carefully remove the weights and bake for an additional 15 minutes. Cool the crust at room temperature for 20 minutes.

4. Pour the cold water into a small bowl and sprinkle the powdered gelatin over it. Set aside to bloom. Put the yogurt in a medium bowl and also set aside.

5. In a small saucepan, combine the cream, sugar, lemon zest, and vanilla. Heat over medium-high heat and stir to dissolve the sugar. When the cream is warm, turn off the heat and stir in the bloomed gelatin. Then pour the cream-and-gelatin mixture over the yogurt and whisk until smooth. Pour the custard into the pie crust and refrigerate for 2 hours.

6. To serve, garnish the tart with the fresh berries. Cut in half, then turn the baking pan 45 degrees and cut each half into thirds for six slices.

BAKING TIP: If you don't have pie weights, a handful of dried rice or dried beans works well as a replacement.

Hazelnut, Chocolate, and Caramel Tart

MAKES 6 SLICES **BAKING VESSEL:** 8-INCH-SQUARE BAKING PAN

Prep Time: 35 minutes, plus 5 hours to chill / **Cook Time:** 35 minutes

When I think of a decadent dessert, I think of chocolate and caramel. This tart (with a no-bake filling) has all that and more.

FOR THE CRUST

Nonstick baking spray

All-purpose flour, for rolling

1 Brown Sugar Butter Pie Crust

FOR THE CARAMEL LAYER

½ cup (113 grams) heavy cream

⅛ teaspoon salt

4 tablespoons (56 grams) unsalted butter

1 cup (200 grams) granulated sugar

¼ cup (56 grams) water

FOR THE CHOCOLATE LAYER

¼ cup (56 grams) heavy cream

2 tablespoons (28 grams) chocolate hazelnut spread, such as Nutella

⅓ cup (53 grams) semisweet chocolate chips

2 tablespoons (16 grams) chopped hazelnuts

¼ teaspoon (1.5 grams) coarse sea salt

TO MAKE THE CRUST

1. Preheat the oven to 375°F. Lightly spray an 8-inch-square baking pan with nonstick baking spray.

2. Sprinkle some flour onto a clean work surface and roll out the dough to a 10-inch square. Flour the rolling pin and work surface as needed. Roll the dough onto the rolling pin and then out onto the baking pan. Press the dough into the corners and sides. Freeze the crust for 10 minutes.

3. Place a piece of parchment paper inside the crust. Add pie weights or a handful of dried rice or dried beans inside. Bake for 20 minutes. Carefully remove the weights and bake for an additional 15 minutes. Cool the crust at room temperature for 20 minutes.

TO MAKE THE CARAMEL LAYER

4. In a small saucepan, combine the cream, salt, and butter over medium heat until the butter has melted. Stir well, remove from the heat, and set aside.

5. In a medium saucepan, combine the sugar and water over medium-high heat. Do not stir. Cook until the sugar begins to turn amber, about 8 minutes. Carefully pour in the cream mixture and stir. The caramel will bubble up, so be careful. Once the cream has been fully incorporated, continue to cook on medium-high heat, stirring constantly, for 2 minutes longer. Pour the caramel filling into the baked pie crust. Refrigerate for 1 hour.

TO MAKE THE CHOCOLATE LAYER

6. In a microwave-safe bowl, heat the cream, chocolate hazelnut spread, and chocolate chips in the microwave in 30-second increments until everything is fully melted. Stir after each increment. When the mixture is smooth, pour it over the chilled caramel filling. Sprinkle the hazelnuts and sea salt on top. Refrigerate for 4 or more hours.

7. To serve, cut in half, then turn the baking pan 45 degrees and cut each half into thirds for six slices.

VARIATION TIP: Try swapping the chocolate hazelnut spread for creamy peanut butter. Use the same amount, and instead of garnishing with hazelnuts, sprinkle on the same quantity of chopped peanuts.

Strawberry Rhubarb Mini Galette

MAKES 6 SLICES **BAKING VESSEL:** SHEET PAN

Prep Time: 20 minutes / **Cook Time:** 35 minutes

A galette is an open-face, free-form pie—no pie tin required! I like galettes because they are foolproof: The more rustic they look, the better. This mini version is the perfect size to produce six slices.

1½ cups (175 grams) quartered fresh strawberries

1½ cups (150 grams) chopped fresh rhubarb

⅓ cup (100 grams) packed light brown sugar

2 tablespoons (25 grams) granulated sugar

1 tablespoon plus 1 teaspoon (10 grams) cornstarch

1 tablespoon (28 grams) lemon juice

½ teaspoon vanilla extract

1 egg

2 tablespoons (28 grams) water

1 [Brown Sugar Butter Pie Crust](#)

All-purpose flour, for rolling

1. Preheat the oven to 375°F. Line a sheet pan with parchment paper.

2. In a large bowl, combine the strawberries, rhubarb, brown sugar, granulated sugar, cornstarch, lemon juice, and vanilla. Toss with a rubber spatula until the fruit is evenly coated.

3. Make the egg wash by whisking the egg and water in a small bowl. Set aside.

4. On a floured surface, roll out the dough to a 10-inch circle. Roll the dough onto the rolling pin and then out onto the prepared sheet pan. Pour the strawberry-rhubarb filling into the center, leaving 2 inches around the sides with no filling. Bring the edges of the dough up over the filling and pinch them to form a sturdy crust. Brush all the visible parts of the dough with egg wash. Freeze the galette on the sheet pan for 5 minutes.

5. Bake for 30 to 35 minutes, or until the filling is bubbly and the dough has evenly browned. Transfer to a serving tray. Cut into six slices and serve immediately.

Mini Pizza Quiche with Pepperoni, Mozzarella, and Olives

MAKES 6 MINI QUICHE **BAKING VESSEL:** MUFFIN TIN

Prep Time: 20 minutes / **Cook Time:** 40 minutes

Pizza and quiche are two very different but equally delicious baked dishes. Why not marry them and create a hearty breakfast at the same time?

Nonstick baking spray

All-purpose flour, for rolling

1 Everything but the Bagel Pie Crust

2 eggs

⅓ cup (67 grams) milk

⅛ teaspoon salt

⅛ teaspoon pepper

2 tablespoons (28 grams) diced pepperoni

2 tablespoons (28 grams) shredded mozzarella cheese

2 tablespoons (28 grams) pitted and sliced black olives

1. Preheat the oven to 375°F. Lightly spray six cups of a muffin tin with nonstick baking spray.

2. Sprinkle some flour onto a clean work surface and roll out the dough to a 10-inch square. Flour the rolling pin and work surface as needed. Use a 4-inch circle cookie cutter to punch out four circles. Gather up the remaining dough and reroll. Punch out two more circles. Fit each circle into a muffin cup. Freeze the mini crusts for 10 minutes.

3. Place a small piece of parchment paper inside each mini crust. Add pie weights or some dried rice or dried beans to each cup. Bake for 15 minutes.

4. While the crusts are baking, in a medium bowl, combine the eggs, milk, salt, and pepper. Whisk until fully blended.

5. When the crusts are done, carefully remove the pie weights. Sprinkle the pepperoni, mozzarella, and black olives evenly over each crust. Pour the egg mixture evenly into each crust. Bake for an additional 25 minutes. Serve immediately.

Mini Bacon and Cheese Quiche

MAKES 6 MINI QUICHE **BAKING VESSEL:** MUFFIN TIN

Prep Time: 25 minutes / **Cook Time:** 40 minutes

Bacon, eggs, and cheese—what more could you ask for in a breakfast? Or lunch? This recipe brings all those ingredients together in mini quiche that are made in a muffin tin and yield six perfect servings. It's enough for one meal for a large family or two meals for a small family. Either way, you'll love every savory bite.

2 strips bacon

Nonstick baking spray

All-purpose flour, for rolling

1 <u>Everything but the Bagel Pie Crust</u>

2 eggs

⅓ cup (67 grams) milk

⅛ teaspoon salt

⅛ teaspoon pepper

¼ cup (58 grams) shredded cheddar cheese

1. Dice the bacon into ¼-inch pieces. Heat a medium skillet on high and cook the bacon until all the fat is fully rendered. Drain off the bacon grease and reserve the bacon bits in a small bowl.

2. Preheat the oven to 375°F. Lightly spray six cups of a muffin tin with nonstick baking spray.

3. Sprinkle some flour onto a clean work surface and roll out the dough into a 10-inch square. Flour the rolling pin and work surface as needed. Use a 4-inch circle cookie cutter to punch out four circles. Gather up the remaining dough and reroll. Punch out two more circles. Fit each circle into a muffin cup. Freeze the mini crusts for 10 minutes.

4. Place a small piece of parchment paper inside each mini crust. Add pie weights or some dried rice or dried beans to each cup. Bake for 15 minutes.

5. While the crusts are baking, in a medium bowl, combine the eggs, milk, salt, and pepper. Whisk until fully blended.

6. When the crusts are done, carefully remove the pie weights. Sprinkle the cheddar and bacon bits evenly over each crust. Pour the egg mixture evenly over the bacon and cheese. Bake for an additional 25 minutes. Serve immediately.

VARIATION TIP: For a vegetarian spin on this quiche, swap out the bacon for broccoli. Chop ½ cup of broccoli into small pieces and sauté with 1 tablespoon of olive oil until tender. Prepare the rest as directed.

Mushroom, Spinach, and Feta Quiche

MAKES 6 SLICES **BAKING VESSEL:** *8-INCH-SQUARE BAKING PAN*

Prep Time: 40 minutes / **Cook Time:** 50 minutes

In my opinion, quiche is the perfect weekend breakfast. I love to mix in vegetables, and the ones in this recipe are my favorites. If mushrooms and spinach aren't your thing, you can switch those out for other vegetables, such as kale, asparagus, and zucchini. Make sure you cook greens down before adding them to the eggs.

1 tablespoon (14 grams) olive oil

2 cups (250 grams) sliced white mushrooms

2 cups (60 grams) fresh spinach

Nonstick baking spray

All-purpose flour, for rolling

1 [Everything but the Bagel Pie Crust](#)

3 eggs

½ cup (113 grams) milk

¼ cup (56 grams) heavy cream

¼ teaspoon (1.5 grams) salt

⅛ teaspoon pepper

¼ cup (37 grams) crumbled feta cheese

1. Heat a large skillet on medium-high heat. Drizzle in the oil and swirl the pan to coat. Add the mushrooms and cook until tender, about 5 minutes. Then add the spinach and cook about 2 minutes more, until the spinach has fully wilted. Transfer to a small bowl and chill in the refrigerator until cooled, 5 to 10 minutes. Once cooled, drain any liquid from the cooked vegetables that has gathered in the bottom of the bowl.

2. Preheat the oven to 375°F. Lightly spray an 8-inch-square baking pan with nonstick baking spray.

3. Sprinkle some flour onto a clean work surface and roll out the dough to a 10-inch square. Flour the rolling pin and work surface as needed. Roll the dough onto the rolling pin and then out onto the baking pan. Press the dough into the corners and sides. Freeze the crust for 10 minutes.

4. Place a piece of parchment paper inside the crust. Add pie weights or a handful of dried rice or dried beans inside. Bake for 20 minutes.

5. While the crust is baking, in a medium bowl, combine the eggs, milk, cream, salt, and pepper. Whisk until fully blended; then add the spinach, mushrooms, and feta cheese.

6. When the crust is done, carefully remove the pie weights. Pour the quiche filling into the crust and bake for an additional 30 minutes.

7. Cool the quiche at room temperature for 10 minutes. Cut in half, and then turn the baking pan 45 degrees and cut each half into thirds for six slices.

BAKING TIP: To get ahead on the prep for this quiche, prepare the crust, form it into the pan the night before, and keep it in the refrigerator until you are ready to serve. Sauté the mushrooms and spinach the night before as well. In the morning, bake the crust, fill it, and bake as directed. A hassle-free morning!

SPICED PUMPKIN CHEESECAKE WITH GINGERSNAP CRUST

CHAPTER 7
puddings *and* cheesecakes

Chocolate Pots de Crème

Classic Vanilla Bean Crème Brûlée

Banana Cream Pudding Parfaits

Tiramisu

No-Bake Mini Vanilla Cheesecakes with Strawberry Compote

Spiced Pumpkin Cheesecake with Gingersnap Crust

Brownie-Bottom Turtle Cheesecake Bars

Butterscotch Pudding

Chocolate Pots de Crème

MAKES 4 SERVINGS

BAKING VESSELS: RAMEKINS, 9-BY-13-INCH BAKING PAN

Prep Time: 25 minutes, plus at least 4 hours to chill / **Cook Time:** 45 minutes

Chocolate makes everything better—am I right? Satisfy that chocolate craving with these decadent pots de crème—a fancy name for baked chocolate pudding. I recommend using a high-quality dark chocolate for this dessert. You really will taste the difference.

1 (4-ounce [113 grams]) dark chocolate bar, chopped

4 egg yolks

1½ cups (360 grams) heavy cream

½ cup (123 grams) milk

¼ cup (50 grams) granulated sugar

⅛ teaspoon salt

½ teaspoon (3 grams) vanilla extract

4 cups (907 grams) hot water

1. Preheat the oven to 300°F. Place four ramekins in a 9-by-13-inch baking pan.

2. Put the dark chocolate in a medium bowl. Put the egg yolks in a separate small bowl.

3. In a small saucepan over medium-high heat, warm the cream, milk, sugar, salt, and vanilla. When the mixture begins to simmer, pour a little bit into the egg yolks while whisking constantly. Then pour the yolk mixture into the saucepan and whisk to combine. Pour the hot custard mixture over the chocolate and let it sit for 1 minute to begin to melt the chocolate. Whisk until the custard is smooth, and then pour it evenly into the ramekins.

4. Carefully pour the hot water into the baking pan to create a water bath around the ramekins, making sure you don't get any water in the custard. Cover the whole baking pan with aluminum foil and poke a few holes into it. Carefully place the baking pan in the oven and bake for 45 minutes.

5. Remove the baking pan from the oven and carefully remove the aluminum foil to release the steam. Be very careful during this step because the steam you're releasing is very hot. Let the ramekins stay in the water bath for 10 minutes; then remove them and put them in the refrigerator for 4 or more hours before serving.

VARIATION TIP: If milk chocolate is more to your liking, feel free to use the same amount of that instead of dark chocolate.

Classic Vanilla Bean Crème Brûlée

MAKES 4 SERVINGS

BAKING VESSELS: RAMEKINS, 9-BY-13-INCH BAKING PAN, SHEET PAN

Prep Time: 15 minutes, plus 8 hours to chill / **Cook Time:** 40 minutes

The word "brûlée" literally means an area of burned-over forest, but for this dessert we're just going to burn the sugar until it is caramelized. This dessert is widely considered a classic and is my father-in-law's favorite, so I make it quite frequently. It's easier than you'd think, so don't feel intimidated. The most important things to remember in making crème brûlée are to get the cream very hot and to not cook the egg yolks.

6 egg yolks

½ cup (100 grams) granulated sugar, plus 4 tablespoons (50 grams)

2 cups (480 grams) heavy cream

½ vanilla bean pod

4 cups (907 grams) hot water

1. Preheat the oven to 300°F. Place four ramekins in a 9-by-13-inch baking pan.

2. In a small bowl, whisk together the egg yolks and ½ cup of sugar.

3. Pour the cream into a medium saucepan and scrape the vanilla beans into the cream. Place the pan over medium-high heat and let the cream steep for 5 minutes. Before it comes to a boil, turn the heat off and pour a little cream into the yolks while whisking constantly. Add the yolk mixture to the saucepan and whisk but do not cook. Then pour the cream evenly into the ramekins.

4. Carefully pour the hot water into the baking pan to create a water bath around the ramekins, making sure you don't get any water in the custard. Cover the whole baking pan with aluminum foil and poke a few holes into it. Carefully place the baking pan in the oven and cook for 40 minutes or until the custard has set and does not appear liquid.

5. Remove the baking pan from the oven and carefully remove the aluminum foil to release the steam. Be very careful during this step because the steam you're releasing is very hot. Place the ramekins on a sheet pan and chill in the refrigerator for at least 8 hours or overnight.

6. To serve, sprinkle 1 tablespoon of sugar over each ramekin. Use a kitchen blowtorch to caramelize the sugar on each ramekin. If you don't have a kitchen blowtorch, you can easily brûlée with your oven broiler: Preheat the broiler. Replace the granulated sugar with brown sugar, sprinkle it over each pudding, and set the ramekins about 2 inches under the broiler for about 2 minutes (watch them and remove them very carefully). Serve immediately.

INGREDIENT TIP: Vanilla bean pods are expensive and tend to dry out. To prolong their shelf life, I store mine in an airtight container in the freezer. If your vanilla bean pod dries out, you can rehydrate it by soaking it in lukewarm water for about an hour.

Banana Cream Pudding Parfaits

MAKES 4 SERVINGS **BAKING VESSEL:** WINEGLASSES (OR RAMEKINS)

Prep Time: 15 minutes, plus 4 hours to chill / **Cook Time:** 10 minutes

I knew I was on the right path in my career when I learned how to make banana cream pudding. It's one of the most satisfying treats, in my opinion, with layers of cream, banana, and cookies. I like to use wineglasses for this recipe because you can see the distinct layers and they make for a beautiful presentation. I make this version using a classic store-bought vanilla wafer, but a good twist would be to use chocolate sandwich cookies. Use the same number of cookies.

FOR THE CUSTARD

3 egg yolks

2 tablespoons (28 grams) unsalted butter, cold

2 cups (480 grams) milk

1 teaspoon (6 grams) vanilla extract

½ cup (100 grams) granulated sugar

2 tablespoons (16 grams) cornstarch

3 small bananas, sliced

1 tablespoon (14 grams) lemon juice

FOR THE PARFAITS

½ cup (120 grams) heavy cream

½ teaspoon (3 grams) vanilla extract

2 tablespoons (14 grams) powdered sugar

32 vanilla wafers

TO MAKE THE CUSTARD

1. Prepare an ice bath by filling a large bowl halfway with ice. Add about 1 cup of water to the ice. Set aside a medium bowl to fit into the ice bath to cool the custard down.

2. Put the egg yolks in a small bowl. Have the cold butter ready.

3. In a small saucepan, combine the milk and vanilla. In a separate bowl, mix the sugar and cornstarch together; then add them to the saucepan. Turn the heat to medium-high and mix with a whisk. When the milk mixture begins to simmer, pour a little hot milk into the yolks while whisking constantly. Pour the yolk mixture into the saucepan and cook until the mixture gets thick, 5 to 8 minutes. When it's thick, remove the pan from the heat and whisk in the butter.

4. When the butter is fully incorporated, pour the custard into the medium bowl you set aside and put the bowl in the ice bath. Stir with a spatula until the custard cools down.

5. Combine the sliced bananas and lemon juice in another medium bowl. Toss with a spatula to coat the bananas in lemon juice. Set aside.

TO FINISH THE PARFAITS

6. Use a handheld electric mixer fitted with a whisk or whisk by hand. In a large bowl, combine the cream, vanilla, and powdered sugar, and whip until stiff peaks form.

7. With your hands, crumble up half the vanilla wafers and place them in the bottom of the wineglasses. Next, distribute the sliced bananas evenly among the wineglasses. Spoon a layer of custard on top of the bananas. Crumble up the remaining vanilla wafers and place on top of the custard. Spoon on the whipped cream last. Chill the parfaits in the refrigerator for at least 4 hours before serving.

INGREDIENT TIP: Coating the bananas in lemon juice in step 5 prevents them from oxidizing and turning brown.

Tiramisu

MAKES 6 SLICES **BAKING VESSEL:** LOAF PAN

Prep Time: 20 minutes, plus 4 hours to chill

I like to think of tiramisu as the cheesecake of Italy. It is creamy and light as air, and the contrasting flavors of mascarpone and coffee are a match made in heaven. A standard tiramisu recipe is made in a 9-by-13-inch baking pan. If you want to double this recipe, use an 8-inch-square baking pan. If you want to triple it, use the standard 9-by-13-inch baking pan.

1 cup (240 grams) heavy cream

1 (8-ounce [226 grams]) package mascarpone cheese

¼ cup (50 grams) granulated sugar

1 teaspoon (6 grams) vanilla extract

1½ cups (354 grams) brewed coffee, cooled

2 tablespoons (28 grams) coffee liqueur (optional)

1 (7-ounce [198 grams]) package ladyfingers

2 tablespoons (15 grams) unsweetened cocoa powder

1. In a stand mixer fitted with the whipping attachment or using a handheld mixer and a large bowl, combine the cream, mascarpone, sugar, and vanilla. Whip until stiff peaks start to form. Set aside.

2. Pour the coffee and coffee liqueur (if using) into a medium bowl. Place half the package of ladyfingers in the coffee mixture, let them soak for 5 seconds, flip them over, and soak them on the other side for 5 seconds. You may need to do this in batches. Line the bottom of the loaf pan with the soaked ladyfingers. Scoop half of the mascarpone custard into the loaf pan. Use the back of a spoon to evenly spread it out.

3. Soak a second layer of ladyfingers and line them up over the layer of custard in the pan. Evenly spread out the rest of the mascarpone custard over this ladyfinger layer.

4. Place the loaf pan on a large sheet of parchment paper. Put the cocoa powder into a sifter or a fine-mesh strainer, and sprinkle it over the surface of the mascarpone. Let the paper catch the wayward cocoa powder; then discard the paper. Put the loaf pan in the refrigerator and chill for at least 4 hours before serving.

5. To serve, run a knife down the center of the pan lengthwise, and then turn the pan 45 degrees and cut into thirds widthwise, yielding six portions of tiramisu.

INGREDIENT TIP: If coffee isn't your thing, give Earl Grey tea a try. Simply swap out the brewed coffee and coffee liqueur in this recipe for 1½ cups (354 grams) of freshly brewed and cooled Earl Grey.

No-Bake Mini Vanilla Cheesecakes with Strawberry Compote

MAKES 6 MINI CAKES **BAKING VESSEL:** MUFFIN TIN

Prep Time: 30 minutes, plus 4 hours to chill / **Cook Time:** 10 minutes

This cheesecake is a perfect treat for hot summer days because there's no baking required, so no need to turn on your oven. The compote will still be warm when you put it on the cheesecake, but don't worry—a hot topping will set nicely on a chilled cheesecake. The strawberries can be switched up for any berry of your choosing; just substitute the same amount.

FOR THE CRUST

½ cup (60 grams) graham cracker crumbs (half a sleeve)

2 tablespoons (28 grams) unsalted butter, melted

1 tablespoon (13 grams) packed light brown sugar

Pinch salt

FOR THE CHEESECAKE

¾ cup (90 grams) cream cheese, at room temperature

2 tablespoons granulated sugar

½ teaspoon vanilla extract

¼ cup heavy cream

FOR THE STRAWBERRY COMPOTE

1 cup (130 grams) hulled and quartered fresh strawberries

1 tablespoon (14 grams) lemon juice

2 tablespoons (56 grams) granulated sugar

1 teaspoon (2 grams) cornstarch

TO MAKE THE CRUST

1. Line a muffin tin with six cupcake liners.

2. In a small bowl, combine the graham cracker crumbs, melted butter, brown sugar, and salt. Mix with a spoon until the crumbs are evenly coated. Spoon the graham cracker mixture into the cupcake liners and press down with the spoon to create an even layer. Set aside.

TO MAKE THE CHEESECAKE

3. In a bowl of a stand mixer fitted with the paddle attachment or using a handheld mixer with a medium bowl, combine the cream cheese, sugar, vanilla, and cream. Mix on medium-high speed until the mixture is very smooth, scraping down the sides as needed.

4. Transfer the cream cheese mixture to a piping bag (no tip needed) or a zip-top bag. When you're ready to pipe, simply cut a 1-inch opening in the bag.

5. Pipe the cheesecake on top of the graham cracker base in each cupcake liner, filling it nearly all the way to the top. Use the back of a spoon to even out the cheesecake in the cupcake liners. Refrigerate while you're preparing the strawberry compote.

TO MAKE THE STRAWBERRY COMPOTE

6. In a small saucepan, combine the strawberries and lemon juice. In a separate small bowl, mix together the sugar and cornstarch; then add it to the strawberries. Mix everything with a spatula. Turn the heat on high and cook, while stirring, until the strawberries have cooked down and the sauce appears thickened, 5 to 8 minutes.

7. Cool the strawberry compote for 5 minutes. Then spoon the compote on top of each mini cheesecake. Chill for 4 or more hours before serving.

VARIATION TIP: Chocolate sandwich cookies make a great cookie crust option for this cheesecake. Swap out the graham cracker crumbs for 6 chocolate sandwich cookies. Either use a food processor to turn them into crumbs or put the cookies in a sealed bag and roll over them with a rolling pin. Use the same amount of melted butter, sugar, and salt as indicated in the ingredients list.

Spiced Pumpkin Cheesecake with Gingersnap Crust

MAKES 6 SLICES **BAKING VESSEL:** 8-INCH-SQUARE BAKING PAN

Prep Time: 15 minutes, plus 8 hours to chill / **Cook Time:** 45 minutes

When summer starts fading away and I begin to feel the cold weather that fall brings, I start to crave pumpkin. There's something about the warm spices that go with pumpkin that perfectly complement the cooler weather. It's such a seasonal staple for me that I couldn't in good conscience write a cookbook without adding in a few great pumpkin desserts. And pumpkin cheesecake is one of the best.

FOR THE CRUST

Nonstick baking spray

30 gingersnap cookies

⅛ teaspoon salt

2 tablespoons (25 grams) packed light brown sugar

4 tablespoons (57 grams) unsalted butter, melted

FOR THE CHEESECAKE

2 (8-ounce [532 grams]) blocks cream cheese, at room temperature

½ cup (50 grams) granulated sugar

¼ teaspoon (1.5 grams) salt

1 teaspoon (2 grams) cinnamon

½ teaspoon (1 gram) ground ginger

¼ teaspoon ground cardamom

⅛ teaspoon ground cloves

½ cup (122 grams) pumpkin puree

3 eggs

TO MAKE THE CRUST

1. Preheat the oven to 350°F. Lightly spray an 8-inch-square baking pan with nonstick baking spray. Line the pan with parchment paper so it comes 2 inches up the sides.

2. In a food processor, combine the gingersnap cookies, salt, and brown sugar. Process until you have fine crumbles. Alternatively, put the cookies in a sealed bag, roll over them with a rolling pin, and then transfer to a medium bowl. Drizzle in the melted butter. Pour the mixture into the baking pan and use the back of a spoon to pack the crust down evenly into the pan. Bake the crust for 10 minutes.

TO MAKE THE CHEESECAKE

3. In a stand mixer fitted with the paddle attachment or using a handheld mixer with a large bowl, combine the cream cheese and sugar, and mix on medium speed. Scrape down the sides as needed and mix until smooth. Add the salt, cinnamon, ginger, cardamom, and cloves, and mix until well incorporated. Add the pumpkin and eggs last, and mix until well incorporated.

4. Pour the cheesecake filling over the hot crust. Reduce the oven temperature to 325°F and bake the cheesecake for 30 to 35 minutes, or until set.

5. Put the baked cheesecake in the refrigerator and chill for at least 8 hours or overnight.

6. To serve, run a knife down the center of the cheesecake to cut it in half. Turn the pan 45 degrees and cut each half into thirds, yielding six slices of cheesecake.

BAKING TIP: To make this cheesecake even more decadent, try topping it with some homemade whipped cream. Whip ½ cup (120 grams) of heavy cream with 2 tablespoons (14 grams) of powdered sugar and 1 teaspoon (6 grams) of vanilla extract. Whip by hand or with a handheld electric mixer until stiff peaks form. Top each slice of cheesecake with whipped cream and serve.

Brownie-Bottom Turtle Cheesecake Bars

MAKES 6 BARS **BAKING VESSEL:** LOAF PAN

Prep Time: 20 minutes, plus 4 hours to chill / **Cook Time:** 45 minutes

While this brownie-bottom cheesecake may seem challenging to make, it will give you serious baking street (kitchen?) cred. The brownie acts as the crust here and is the perfect chocolate note to pair with the creamy cheesecake filling, which is topped with chocolate chips, crunchy pecans, and caramel sauce. You may need a glass of milk with this one.

FOR THE BROWNIE LAYER

Nonstick baking spray

⅓ cup (63 grams) semisweet chocolate chips

4 tablespoons (57 grams) unsalted butter

1 egg

¼ cup (50 grams) granulated sugar

¼ teaspoon (1.5 grams) salt

¼ cup (34 grams) all-purpose flour

FOR THE CHEESECAKE LAYER

2 (8-ounce [532 grams]) blocks cream cheese, at room temperature

½ cup (100 grams) granulated sugar

1 egg

1 teaspoon (6 grams) vanilla extract

¼ cup (28 grams) chopped pecans

¼ cup (40 grams) semisweet chocolate chips

¼ cup (85 grams) store-bought caramel sauce

TO MAKE THE BROWNIE LAYER

1. Preheat the oven to 350°F. Lightly spray a loaf pan with nonstick baking spray, and then line it with parchment paper so it comes 2 inches up the sides.

2. In a microwave-safe bowl, combine the chocolate chips and butter. Microwave in 30-second increments until they're fully melted, stirring after each increment. Whisk in the egg, sugar, salt, and flour. Whisk until the mixture is smooth and no flour chunks are visible. Pour the batter into the loaf pan and bake for 10 minutes while you're preparing the cheesecake layer.

TO MAKE THE CHEESECAKE LAYER

3. In the bowl of a stand mixer fitted with the paddle attachment or using a handheld mixer with a large bowl, combine the cream cheese and sugar. Mix on medium speed, scraping down the sides as needed, until smooth. Add the egg and vanilla and mix until well incorporated.

4. After the brownie has baked for 10 minutes, remove the loaf pan from the oven and pour the cheesecake batter over the brownie. Use a spoon to spread the cheesecake layer evenly in the pan. Sprinkle the pecans and chocolate chips evenly over the surface.

5. Reduce the oven temperature to 325°F and bake for 35 minutes. Remove from the oven and chill in the refrigerator for at least 4 hours.

6. To serve, drizzle the caramel sauce over the top of the cheesecake. Run a knife down the center of the cheesecake to cut it in half. Turn the pan 45 degrees and cut the halves into thirds, yielding six cheesecake bars.

Butterscotch Pudding

MAKES 4 SERVINGS **BAKING VESSEL:** RAMEKINS

Prep Time: 20 minutes, plus 4 hours to chill

Combining cream, brown sugar, and butter is a one-way ticket to flavor-town. Some people love the classic flavor of butterscotch, but there are ways to kick it up if you're in the mood for something more. Try adding ½ teaspoon (3 grams) more salt in step 1 to make your taste buds really pop. To give this pudding a boozy boost, add 1 tablespoon (14 grams) of spiced dark rum with the milk and cream in step 1. For a berry twist, add 1 tablespoon (14 grams) of raspberry jam with the milk and cream.

4 egg yolks

4 tablespoons (57 grams) unsalted butter, cold, cubed

1 cup (240 grams) heavy cream

1 cup (240 grams) milk

½ teaspoon (3 grams) salt

1 teaspoon (6 grams) vanilla extract

2 tablespoons (7 grams) cornstarch

1 cup (200 grams) packed light brown sugar

1. Put the egg yolks in a small bowl and set aside. Have the cold butter ready.

2. In a small saucepan, combine the cream, milk, salt, and vanilla. Mix the cornstarch and brown sugar together in a small bowl, and then add the mixture to the saucepan. Turn the heat to medium-high and stir until the cream mixture and cornstarch mixture are well incorporated. Once the cream starts to simmer, pour a little hot cream into the yolks while whisking constantly. Then pour the yolk mixture into the saucepan and cook, stirring constantly, until the custard starts to thicken up, 8 to 10 minutes.

3. Remove the pan from the heat and stir in the butter. When all the butter is incorporated, pour the custard into four ramekins. Place a small piece of plastic wrap directly on the surface of each pudding, and then put the ramekins in the refrigerator. Chill for at least 4 hours before serving.

BAKING TIP: This pudding can be made up to 1 week in advance. Keep the plastic wrap on until you are ready to serve.

BLUEBERRY THYME TURNOVERS

CHAPTER 8
turnovers and **pastries**

Cinnamon Apple Turnovers

Blueberry Thyme Turnovers

Egg and Cheese Breakfast Turnovers

Cremini Mushroom, Thyme, and Gruyère Turnovers

Cinnamon Rolls

Apricot and Raspberry Jam Kolaches

Easy Kouign-Amann

Brie, Fig, and Pine Nut Danish

Cinnamon Apple Turnovers

MAKES 6 TURNOVERS **BAKING VESSEL:** SHEET PAN

Prep Time: 20 minutes, plus 30 minutes to chill / **Cook Time:** 20 minutes

Cinnamon is one of those smells that spreads through the whole house and entices you into the kitchen. This recipe is great because you likely already have these ingredients on hand, and it makes for a perfect sweet treat. I prefer using a green apple in my baked apple recipes because I like the tartness, but I encourage you to use any apple variety you prefer.

1 large (138 grams) green apple, peeled, cored, and diced

¼ cup (50 grams) packed light brown sugar

½ teaspoon (1 gram) ground cinnamon

Pinch salt

2 teaspoons (5 grams) cornstarch

1 tablespoon (14 grams) lemon juice

1 tablespoon (14 grams) unsalted butter

1 egg

2 tablespoons (28 grams) water

All-purpose flour, for rolling

1 Brown Sugar Butter Pie Crust

1. In a medium bowl, combine the apple, brown sugar, cinnamon, salt, cornstarch, and lemon juice, and toss with a spatula until the fruit is evenly coated.

2. Melt the butter in a medium saucepan on medium-high heat. Add the apple mixture and cook, stirring, until the apples have softened and the sauce appears thick, about 5 minutes. Transfer the apple mixture to a small bowl and chill in the refrigerator until it is cool, about 20 minutes.

3. Preheat the oven to 425°F. Line a sheet pan with parchment paper.

4. In a small bowl, whisk together the egg and water. Set aside.

5. On a lightly floured work surface, roll out the pie dough to 8 by 12 inches. Cut in half lengthwise and then in thirds widthwise. This should yield six 4-inch squares. Use a pastry brush to brush the egg wash over the edges of each piece of dough. Place 1 tablespoon of apple filling in the center of a piece of dough. Fold two opposite corners of dough together to create a triangle and press to seal. Use a fork to crimp the edges together. Repeat this process with the remaining squares of dough. Brush the remaining egg wash over the top surface of all the turnovers. Use a fork to poke a few holes in each one. Freeze the turnovers on the sheet pan for 10 minutes.

6. Bake the turnovers for 18 to 20 minutes, or until they're evenly browned.

VARIATION TIP: Pears work well as a variation in this recipe. Simply substitute the same quantity and prepare as directed. My favorite baking pear is the Bosc, but D'Anjou and Comice pears are also great for baking.

Blueberry Thyme Turnovers

MAKES 6 TURNOVERS **BAKING VESSEL:** SHEET PAN

Prep Time: 20 minutes, plus 30 minutes to chill / **Cook Time:** 20 minutes

My signature baking style is to use fresh herbs whenever possible. Thyme has a fruity floral fragrance, and because of that, I like to pair it with berries. I sometimes prepare these turnovers and store them uncooked in the freezer. Whenever I want a quick treat, I just pull one or two out and bake them from frozen at the step indicated in the recipe.

1 pint (6 ounces [170 grams]) fresh blueberries

2 teaspoons (1 gram) chopped fresh thyme

1 teaspoon (2 grams) lemon zest

1 tablespoon (14 grams) lemon juice

2 tablespoons (25 grams) granulated sugar

½ teaspoon (3 grams) vanilla extract

1½ teaspoon (4 grams) cornstarch

1 egg

2 tablespoons (28 grams) water

All-purpose flour, for rolling

1 Brown Sugar Butter Pie Crust

1. In a medium bowl, combine the blueberries, thyme, lemon zest, lemon juice, sugar, vanilla, and cornstarch, and toss with a spatula until the fruit is evenly coated. Add the blueberry mixture to a medium saucepan and cook on high heat while stirring, until the blueberries have broken down and the sauce appears thick, about 5 minutes. Transfer the blueberries to a small bowl and chill in the refrigerator until fully cooled, about 20 minutes.

2. In a small bowl, whisk the egg and water together. Set aside.

3. Preheat the oven to 425°F. Line a sheet pan with parchment paper.

4. On a lightly floured work surface, roll out the pie dough to 8 by 12 inches. Cut in half lengthwise and then in thirds widthwise. This should yield six 4-inch squares. Use a pastry brush to brush the egg wash over the edges of each piece of dough. Place 1 tablespoon of blueberry filling in the center of a piece of dough. Fold two opposite corners of dough together to create a triangle and press to seal. Use a fork to crimp the edges together. Repeat this process with the remaining squares of dough. Brush the remaining egg wash over the top surface of all the turnovers. Use a fork to poke a few holes in each one. Freeze the turnovers on the sheet pan for 10 minutes.

5. Bake the turnovers for 18 to 20 minutes, or until they're evenly browned.

VARIATION TIP: Another favorite flavor combination of mine is cranberry and rosemary. Swap blueberries and thyme for a pint (170 grams) of fresh cranberries and 2 teaspoons (1 gram) of chopped fresh rosemary. Prepare the recipe the same way.

Egg and Cheese Breakfast Turnovers

MAKES 6 TURNOVERS **BAKING VESSEL:** SHEET PAN

Prep Time: 20 minutes, plus 30 minutes to chill / **Cook Time:** 20 minutes

These egg and cheese turnovers are proof that breakfast doesn't have to be boring. They are also a perfect on-the-go breakfast to make ahead for those busy weeks. After they're cooked, keep them in the freezer and reheat in a 400°F oven for 5 minutes for a quick meal.

1 teaspoon (4 grams) olive oil

3 eggs, divided

⅛ teaspoon salt

⅛ teaspoon pepper

¼ cup (57 grams) shredded cheddar cheese

2 tablespoons (28 grams) water

All-purpose flour, for rolling

1 Everything but the Bagel Pie Crust

1. Heat a large skillet on medium heat. Pour in the olive oil, then crack in two eggs. Sprinkle with the salt and pepper and stir with a spatula to scramble the eggs in the skillet. When the eggs are cooked to your liking, transfer them to a small bowl and add the cheddar cheese. Toss with a spatula to begin to melt the cheese. Chill in the refrigerator until fully cooled, about 20 minutes.

2. In a small bowl, whisk the remaining egg and the water together. Set aside.

3. Preheat the oven to 425°F. Line a sheet pan with parchment paper.

4. On a lightly floured work surface, roll out the pie dough to 8 by 12 inches. Cut in half lengthwise and then in thirds widthwise. This should yield six 4-inch squares. Use a pastry brush to brush the egg wash over the edges of each piece of dough. Place 1 tablespoon of egg filling in the center of a piece of dough. Fold two opposite corners of dough together to create a triangle and press to seal. Use a fork to crimp the edges together. Repeat this process with the remaining squares of dough. Brush the remaining egg wash over the top surface of all the turnovers. Use a fork to poke a few holes in each one. Freeze the turnovers on the sheet pan for 10 minutes.

5. Bake the turnovers for 18 to 20 minutes, or until they're evenly browned.

VARIATION TIP: For a spicy version, you can add some heat to your turnovers by mincing 1 tablespoon of fresh jalapeño pepper and adding it to your scrambled eggs during step 2.

Cremini Mushroom, Thyme, and Gruyère Turnovers

MAKES 6 TURNOVERS **BAKING VESSEL:** SHEET PAN

Prep Time: 20 minutes, plus 30 minutes to chill / **Cook Time:** 20 minutes

When I'm not baking desserts, chances are I'm experimenting with some savory food. I love all vegetables, but mushrooms are probably my favorite. Cremini mushrooms are actually young portabella mushrooms, which is why they're sometimes also called baby bellas.

2 teaspoons (9 grams) olive oil

2 cups (123 grams) sliced cremini mushrooms

1 teaspoon chopped fresh thyme

¼ teaspoon (1.5 grams) salt

⅛ teaspoon pepper

1 teaspoon (2 grams) all-purpose flour, plus more for rolling

2 tablespoons (28 grams) vegetable stock or water

⅓ cup (78 grams) shredded Gruyère cheese

1 egg

2 tablespoons (28 grams) water

1 Everything but the Bagel Pie Crust

1. Heat a small saucepan on medium-high heat. Once the saucepan is warmed up, pour in the olive oil, then add the mushrooms and thyme. Add the salt and pepper and stir with a spatula. Once the mushrooms have softened a little, about 3 minutes, sprinkle in the flour and toss with a spatula to evenly coat the mushrooms. Add the vegetable stock and cook for about 3 minutes. The sauce around the mushrooms should appear thick. Transfer to a small bowl and sprinkle in the Gruyère. Toss with a spatula until well combined and the cheese begins to melt. Chill in the refrigerator until fully cooled, about 20 minutes.

2. In a small bowl, whisk the egg and water together. Set aside.

3. Line a sheet pan with parchment paper. Preheat the oven to 425°F.

4. On a lightly floured work surface, roll out the pie dough to 8 by 12 inches. Cut in half lengthwise and then in thirds widthwise. This should yield six 4-inch squares. Use a pastry brush to brush the egg wash over the edges of each piece of dough. Place 1 tablespoon of mushroom filling in the center of a piece of dough. Fold two opposite corners of dough together to create a triangle and press to seal. Use a fork to crimp the edges together. Repeat this process with the remaining squares of dough. Brush the remaining egg wash over the top surface of all the turnovers. Use a fork to poke a few holes in each one. Freeze the turnovers on the sheet pan for 10 minutes.

5. Bake the turnovers for 18 to 20 minutes, or until they're evenly browned.

BAKING TIP: Turnovers bake best when the dough is cold. It's important to chill the butter in the dough before it goes into the oven, or the turnover may not hold its shape.

Cinnamon Rolls

MAKES 6 ROLLS **BAKING VESSEL:** 8-INCH-SQUARE BAKING PAN

Prep Time: 25 minutes, plus 1 hour 30 minutes to rise / **Cook Time:** 25 minutes

If you want to free up more time in the morning, make the dough the night before. Follow the directions through step 6; then, instead of letting the dough rise the second time (as described at the end of the step), leave it covered in the refrigerator overnight. The next morning, all you have to do is make the icing and bake the dough. Be sure to ice these as soon as they come out of the oven so the cream cheese icing melts a little bit into the rolls.

FOR THE CINNAMON ROLLS

½ cup (113 grams) milk

2¼ teaspoons (7 grams) active dry yeast (1 package)

Nonstick baking spray or canola oil

2 cups plus 2 tablespoons (270 grams) all-purpose flour, plus more for rolling

¼ teaspoon (1.5 grams) salt

¼ cup (50 grams) granulated sugar

1 egg

¼ cup (56 grams) unsalted butter, at room temperature

¼ cup (50 grams) packed light brown sugar

2 teaspoons (5 grams) cinnamon

FOR THE ICING

2 tablespoons (28 grams) cream cheese, at room temperature

2 tablespoons (28 grams) unsalted butter, at room temperature

¼ cup (25 grams) powdered sugar

½ teaspoon (3 grams) vanilla extract

1 tablespoon (14 grams) milk

TO MAKE THE CINNAMON ROLLS

1. In a microwave-safe bowl, heat the milk on high for 30 seconds to 1 minute until it's lukewarm. Sprinkle the yeast over it and let it sit for 5 minutes.

2. Lightly grease a medium bowl and an 8-inch-square baking pan with nonstick baking spray.

3. In the bowl of a stand mixer fitted with the dough hook or using a handheld mixer and a large bowl, combine the flour, salt, and granulated sugar. Pour in the yeast mixture and mix on medium speed. Add the egg and then the butter, and mix until combined. The dough should pull away from the sides of the bowl but will be tacky. Transfer the dough to the greased bowl, cover with plastic wrap, and let rise at room temperature for 1 hour.

4. In a small bowl, combine the brown sugar and cinnamon and mix with a fork. Set aside.

5. Roll out the dough on a floured work surface to a 10-inch square. Sprinkle the cinnamon-and-brown-sugar mixture over it, leaving a ½-inch border around the edges.

6. Roll the dough up tightly from the bottom to the top, and pinch the edges closed. Cut the roll in half, and then cut each half into thirds. Place the cinnamon rolls in the prepared baking pan. Cover with plastic wrap and let rise at room temperature for 30 minutes.

7. Preheat the oven to 350°F.

8. Bake the cinnamon rolls for 22 minutes, or until they're evenly browned.

TO MAKE THE ICING

9. Combine the cream cheese, butter, and powdered sugar in a medium bowl. Mix together with a rubber spatula until smooth. Stir in the vanilla and then the milk, and mix until smooth.

10. Immediately ice the cinnamon rolls when they come out of the oven. Use a spatula to evenly spread the icing over the tops. Serve immediately.

BAKING TIP: Cutting cinnamon roll dough with a knife can be challenging. For an easier cut, use a piece of dental floss. Wiggle the center of the floss underneath the roll of dough, bring both ends up over the dough, cross the ends, and pull, making a clean cut.

Apricot and Raspberry Jam Kolaches

MAKES 6 KOLACHES **BAKING VESSEL:** 8-INCH-SQUARE BAKING PAN

Prep Time: 20 minutes, plus 2 hours 30 minutes to rise / **Cook Time:** 20 minutes

Kolaches are a type of pastry that originated as a wedding dessert in Central Europe and are now gaining popularity in the rest of Europe and in the United States. They are made of a rich, sweet dough filled with fruity jam; I like to think of them as a sort of donut–Danish cross.

⅓ cup (67 grams) milk

1 teaspoon (3 grams) active dry yeast

Nonstick baking spray or canola oil

1 cup (120 grams) all-purpose flour

1 tablespoon (12 grams) granulated sugar

¼ teaspoon (1.5 grams) salt

2 tablespoons (28 grams) unsalted butter, melted

1 egg yolk

1 egg

2 tablespoons (28 grams) water

3 tablespoons (60 grams) raspberry jam

3 tablespoons (60 grams) apricot jam

1. In a microwave-safe bowl, heat the milk on high for 30 seconds to 1 minute until it's lukewarm. Sprinkle the yeast over it and let it sit for 5 minutes.

2. Lightly grease a medium bowl and an 8-inch-square baking pan with nonstick baking spray.

3. In a medium bowl, combine the flour, sugar, and salt. Pour in the yeast mixture and stir with a spatula. Pour in the melted butter and egg yolk. Mix with a spatula until no dry bits remain. Transfer the dough to a clean work surface and knead by hand for 5 minutes, until the dough is smooth. Put the dough in the greased bowl and cover with plastic wrap. Let rise at room temperature for 1½ hours.

4. Divide the dough into six equal pieces. You can either eyeball it or use a kitchen scale. Roll each piece of dough into a ball and place it in the prepared baking pan. Cover with plastic wrap and let rise again at room temperature for 1 hour.

5. Preheat the oven to 375°F.

6. Mix the egg wash by whisking the egg and water together in a small bowl.

7. Use your thumb to make an indent in the center of each ball of dough. Fill three pieces of dough with 1 tablespoon of raspberry jam each. Fill the remaining three pieces of dough with 1 tablespoon of apricot jam each. Brush each piece of dough with egg wash.

8. Bake the kolaches for 18 minutes, or until they're evenly browned. Cool at room temperature for 5 minutes before serving.

VARIATION TIP: If you want to switch up the flavors of jam, go right ahead! Each kolache should be filled with 1 tablespoon (20 grams) of filling—cherry, blackberry, strawberry, and plum jams are all great alternatives.

Easy Kouign-Amann

MAKES 6 KOUIGN-AMANN **BAKING VESSEL:** MUFFIN TIN

Prep Time: 25 minutes, plus 35 minutes to chill and 1 hour to rise /
Cook Time: 30 minutes

Pronounced qween-ah-MON, this famously indulgent French pastry is what I think of as a caramelized croissant. It's a yeasted dough, laminated like a biscuit to create layers upon layers, and then rolled in sugar. When baked, it produces a crispy, caramelized pastry.

¼ cup (56 grams) water

1 teaspoon (3 grams) active dry yeast

1 cup (120 grams) all-purpose flour, plus more for rolling

¾ teaspoon (4.5 grams) salt, divided

7 tablespoons (99 grams) unsalted butter, cold, cubed

¼ cup (50 grams) granulated sugar

Nonstick baking spray

1. In a microwave-safe bowl, heat the water on high for 20 seconds until it's lukewarm. Sprinkle the yeast over it and let it sit for 5 minutes.

2. In the bowl of a stand mixer fitted with a paddle attachment or using a handheld mixer and a large bowl, combine the flour and ½ teaspoon (3 grams) of salt. Add the cold cubed butter and mix on low. Do not mix the butter fully in—you want to keep large visible chunks of butter. Add the yeast mixture and continue to mix on low until a dough forms. Turn the mixer off and use your hands to form the dough into a ball. Wrap it in plastic wrap and chill in the refrigerator for 30 minutes.

3. Roll out the dough on a floured work surface into a 10-inch square. Take one-third of the dough from the left and fold it into the center. Take one-third from the right and fold it over the left flap, creating a book fold. Roll out the dough again to a 10-inch square and repeat the folds. Repeat once more, for a total of three times. After the third fold, put the dough on a sheet pan and chill in the freezer for 5 minutes.

4. In a small bowl, combine the remaining ¼ teaspoon (1.5 grams) of salt and the sugar. Sprinkle your work surface with the sugar mixture. Take dough from the freezer and roll it into the sugar, flipping it over once to coat both sides in sugar. Roll out the dough into an 8-by-12-inch rectangle. Cut it in half lengthwise and then in thirds widthwise, yielding six 4-inch squares.

5. Spray six cups of a muffin tin with nonstick baking spray. Place each square into the center of a cup and pinch the four corners together at the top. Cover the whole tin loosely with plastic wrap and let rise at room temperature for 1 hour.

6. Preheat the oven to 425°F.

7. Bake the kouign-amann for 10 minutes; then reduce the heat to 350°F and bake for an additional 20 minutes. Use a fork to help remove the kouign-amann from the muffin tin, and place on a wire rack to cool at room temperature for 10 minutes before serving.

BAKING TIP: It's important for the dough to stay cold while doing the book folds. If your kitchen is warm, freeze the dough for 5 minutes in between folds during step 3.

Brie, Fig, and Pine Nut Danish

MAKES 6 DANISH **BAKING VESSEL:** SHEET PAN

Prep Time: 25 minutes, plus 35 minutes to chill and 1 hour to rise / **Cook Time:** 20 minutes

Baked Brie wrapped in puff pastry is a classic appetizer, and that's exactly what inspired this Danish. I could eat this combination of flavors every day and be a happy camper. Fig is my favorite fruit to pair it with, but other great pairings would be raspberries or blackberries. One berry for each Danish will do.

¼ cup (56 grams) water

1 teaspoon (3 grams) active dry yeast

1 cup (120 grams) all-purpose flour

½ teaspoon (3 grams) salt

7 tablespoons (99 grams) unsalted butter, cold, cubed

4 ounces (113 grams) Brie cheese, sliced into 6 (¼-inch) pieces

3 fresh figs, cut in half

2 tablespoons (18 grams) chopped pine nuts

1. In a microwave-safe bowl, heat the water on high for 20 seconds until it's lukewarm. Sprinkle the yeast over it and let it sit for 5 minutes.

2. In the bowl of a stand mixer fitted with the paddle attachment or using a handheld mixer and a large bowl, combine the flour and salt. Add the cold cubed butter and mix on low. Do not mix the butter in completely—you want to keep large visible chunks of butter. Add the yeast mixture and continue to mix on low until a dough forms. Turn off the mixer and use your hands to form the dough into a ball. Wrap it in plastic wrap and chill in the refrigerator for 30 minutes.

3. Roll out the dough on a floured work surface into a 10-inch square. Take one-third of the dough from the left and fold it into the center. Take one-third from the right and fold it over the left flap, creating a book fold. Roll out the dough again to a 10-inch square and repeat the folds. Repeat once more, for a total of three times. After the third fold, place the dough on a sheet pan and chill it in the freezer for 5 minutes.

4. Line a sheet pan with parchment paper. Roll out the dough into an 8-by-12-inch rectangle. Cut it in half lengthwise and then in thirds widthwise, yielding six 4-inch squares. Place the squares on the sheet pan, spaced out 1 inch apart. Take a fork and prick the center of each square so the danish don't puff up, leaving a ½-inch border all around. Place a piece of Brie in the center of each square. Place half of a fig next to the cheese and sprinkle some chopped pine nuts on top. Repeat with each danish. Cover the whole pan with plastic wrap and let rise at room temperature for 1 hour.

5. Preheat the oven to 400°F.

6. Bake the danish for 20 minutes, turning the pan halfway through.

INGREDIENT TIP: Fresh figs can sometimes be hard to find. Dried figs will work just as well in this recipe. Use six large pieces of dried fig—one for each danish—and prepare as directed.

measurement conversions

	US STANDARD	US STANDARD (OUNCES)	METRIC (APPROXIMATE)
VOLUME EQUIVALENTS (LIQUID)	2 tablespoons	1 fl. oz.	30 mL
	¼ cup	2 fl. oz.	60 mL
	½ cup	4 fl. oz.	120 mL
	1 cup	8 fl. oz.	240 mL
	1½ cups	12 fl. oz.	355 mL
	2 cups or 1 pint	16 fl. oz.	475 mL
	4 cups or 1 quart	32 fl. oz.	1 L
	1 gallon	128 fl. oz.	4 L
VOLUME EQUIVALENTS (DRY)	⅛ teaspoon	—	0.5 mL
	¼ teaspoon	—	1 mL
	½ teaspoon	—	2 mL
	¾ teaspoon	—	4 mL
	1 teaspoon	—	5 mL
	1 tablespoon	—	15 mL
	¼ cup	—	59 mL
	⅓ cup	—	79 mL
	½ cup	—	118 mL
	⅔ cup	—	156 mL
	¾ cup	—	177 mL
	1 cup	—	235 mL
	2 cups or 1 pint	—	475 mL
	3 cups	—	700 mL
	4 cups or 1 quart	—	1 L
	½ gallon	—	2 L
	1 gallon	—	4 L
WEIGHT EQUIVALENTS	½ ounce	—	15 g
	1 ounce	—	30 g
	2 ounces	—	60 g
	4 ounces	—	115 g
	8 ounces	—	225 g
	12 ounces	—	340 g
	16 ounces or 1 pound	—	455 g

	FAHRENHEIT (F)	CELSIUS (C) (APPROXIMATE)
OVEN TEMPERATURES	250°F	120°C
	300°F	150°C
	325°F	180°C
	375°F	190°C
	400°F	200°C
	425°F	220°C
	450°F	230°C

Printed in Dunstable, United Kingdom